Poetry Without Pants

Written When Nobody's Looking

Volume 2 of the ShiftPoetry Collection

EDITED BY
Barbara Ligeti & Howard Kern

Poetry without Pants:
Written when Nobody's Looking

EDITED BY Barbara Ligeti and Howard Kern

© 2020 by Mindful Media LLC

All rights reserved. No part of this book may be reproduced in any form or by any electronic or mechanical means, including information storage and retrieval systems, without permission in writing from the publisher, except by a reviewer, who may quote brief passages in a review. For permissions, please write to address below or email barbaraligeti@mac.com. Any members of education institutions wishing to photocopy or electronically reproduce part or all of the work for classroom use, or publishers who would like to obtain permission to include the work in an anthology, should send their inquiries to ShiftPoetry™ c/o Barbara Ligeti, 910 West End Avenue—Suite 6F, New York, NY 10025.

ISBN 978-1-7348787-2-1 (trade paperback original)

First edition published November 2020

BISAC category code
SEL027000: Self-Help/Personal Growth/Success

COVER AND BOOK DESIGN:
KG Design International
www.katgeorges.com
kgeokat@mac.com

Mindful Media LLC
910 West End Avenue—Suite 6F
New York, NY 10025
www.ShiftPoetry.com
info@shiftpoetry.com

Dedicated to

all teachers who have, during the pandemic, zoomed wellness experiences into our living rooms, from hatha yoga and kundalini classes, to Pilates instruction, to Thai massage restorative sessions, to ecstatic dance, breath work and meditation. They've opened their private studios and homes and drawn us in to emulate, even re-create, the best centers or gyms we have ever experienced.

In particular thanks and love to our generous and glorious
Phoebe Diftler
Pamela Heffler
Linh James aka Guru Mitar
Grace Kono-Wells
Rima Thierry
Susan Cambigue Tracey
ShiftPoets All!!

TABLE OF CONTENTS

Foreword .... *i*
Preface .... *ii*
Introduction .... *v*
Editors' Note .... *xi*

PART ONE: THE WORKBOOK: PROMPT-DRIVEN WRITING
Prompts, Space to Write, Poems *1*
Prompt #1: Zoom Wardrobe *2*
Prompt #2: Alone *16*
Prompt #3: Time with Your Pod *24*
Prompt #4: Self Reflections *34*

PART TWO: WRITING WHEN NOBODY'S LOOKING
Highlighted ShiftPoets *47*
Jeffrey Altshuler *48*
Phoebe Diftler *54*
Stefanie D. Fletcher *60*
Robert Galinsky *70*
Pam Heffler *73*
Jeffrey Hollander *78*
Twesigye Jackson Kaguri *82*
Howard Kern *86*
Grace Kono-Wells *94*
Barbara Ligeti *100*
Jenifer Winters O'Neill *109*
Jesse Pudles *114*
Susan Cambigue Tracey *120*
Ruth Waytz *129*
Dennis Webb *132*

PART THREE: SCHTICKPOETRY
Satire, Spoof, and Parody *139*

Index *171*
Acknowledgments *173*
About Us *174*

FOREWORD

For the past eight months or so, many of us have been sitting at our desks, conducting business, having meetings, and even forced to visit with friends and family on Zoom or Skype. We're ordering in and shopping online. Our news is coming to us from anchors and reporters working from their basements.

As we've tried to cope with this imposed isolation and separation, most of us can't help but let our minds wander. We daydream, drift into unusual thought patterns and occasionally engage in some sort of magical thinking.

We're facing the world from the waist up. *Poetry without Pants: Written When Nobody's Looking* is a collection of poems and other writings inspired by these conditions. The works in this book are expressive, frequently wry and ironic, often reflecting a more serious subtext and undercurrent. Some address the situation head on. But in the end, they all have one thing in common. They ask us to consider—"What's going on under the desk"—and beyond the view we see on our screens.

Whether you participate in the workshops, or apply the tools when you're alone with your thoughts, the ShiftPoetry approach can help you to dig a little deeper, discover what's truly in your heart and come to terms with your emotions, so you can free yourself to face this "new normal" with a little more joy and contentment.

October, 2020
Jeffrey Altshuler
Screenwriter, Journalist
Founder and Managing Director,
Scenario Magazine

PREFACE

Poetry Without Pants: Written When Nobody's Looking, is the second volume in an evolving series of books created by ShiftPoetry™. Our first book, *ShiftPoetry in the Time of COVID-19: An Anthology of Healing Poems and a Workbook to Help You Write Yourself Well*, was published in May, 2020, as the COVID-19 Pandemic was tightening its grip on the nation and the world.

ShiftPoetry is a workshop-based process of spontaneous and intuitive writing in which the participants "sprint write", usually for ten-minute intervals, in response to thought-provoking and often timely prompts generated by the group's leaders. Originally designed for live, in-person workshops, the sessions have moved into the virtual universe via Zoom.

As time passed, and many ShiftPoetry participants seemed to be developing some acceptance, as well as a sense of humor, about the inevitability of the current situation, the creators felt that another book was in order. They started with the tongue-in-cheek premise and title, *Poetry Without Pants: Written When Nobody's Looking*, put it out to the community as an overall prompt, and asked for contributions.

The responses that were submitted, along with others generated in the regular ShiftPoetry workshops, ranged from classic, introspective ShiftPoems, evoking deep emotions and conceived to help take the writer from dark to light, to works that were more lighthearted. Many were wry, ironic, satirical, or straight up parody. Others described scenes observed outside the writer's window, while some riffed on the relentless drumbeat of the news.

This second book, *Poetry Without Pants*, was originally intended to be a companion piece, a continuum of Volume One,

ShiftPoetry in the Time of COVID-19. Instead it has taken on a life of its own.

The format of this book seems to have naturally fallen into three parts:

- **Part One** is very much like the preceding book, "An anthology of healing poems and a workbook to help you to write yourself well." This section includes specific prompts and poems written in response to those prompts, accompanied by a blank page for the reader to write their own poem or poems in response to the prompt.
- **Part Two** is a collection of the work of a hand-full of our more active and regular ShiftPoets. Each of them has reflected on what has bubbled up in both prompt driven sessions and as a result of their own introspection inspired, of course, by their ShiftPoetry practice.
- **Part Three** has come as something of a surprise, even to the editors. It is a group of poems a little more off-the-wall and outside the parameters of the classical ShiftPoetry offerings. Some of the contributing writers chose to remain anonymous. Some have chosen fanciful noms de plume for this section. Some of the humor approaches being "over the top" or is constructed in innovative and unlikely formats. The ShiftPoetry creators decided to label this last section SchtickPoetry, a collection of work worthy of being read at a Thanksgiving table or on a comedy club stage.

The ShiftPoetry concept was developed by Barbara Ligeti and Howard Kern to inspire people to write freely and spontaneously, in order to feel better about any and all aspects of their lives. Since the organization's inception in 2018, ShiftPoetry workshops have gathered folks in a variety rooms, from the homes of the creators, to yoga studios, meditation centers, classrooms, and civic centers. The objective of the workshops is to offer a fast, fun and inspiring version of "bibliotherapy"—a process of using one's own words to guide participants in discovering personal issues, to bring them to light, write about them without rules, spontaneously and "poetically", and then to let them go, and greet a happier day.

Other forms of bibliotherapy include journaling and memoir writing, but what distinguishes ShiftPoetry in this category is its immediate, spontaneous method of generating words from the heart, while leaving the ego, i.e. the need to cling to self-esteem and self-importance, behind. The process is not judgmental. There is no critique. Whatever you write is perfect.

Before you begin reading and interacting with Part One of this book, please take a look at the Introduction. It contains valuable background information, and a word or two about how best to use this volume.

Meanwhile—know that our overriding purpose is for you is to explore your own thoughts and words to find solutions and happiness. Our wish is for you to write freely and from the heart, in order to generate your own ShiftPoetry and whatever else you're inspired to write to get you through dark times, express joy and gratitude for the good times, and just generally savor life.

INTRODUCTION

A brief history of ShiftPoetry™

In March of 2018, nearly two years to the day before the COVID-19 Pandemic was confirmed by the World Health Organization, two strangers, Barbara Ligeti, a media professional, and Howard Kern, a corporate attorney and writer, met in Vietnam. The two were among 20 folks touring the North and South as part of a Kundalini Yoga retreat hosted by one of their favorite teachers, Guru Mitar, aka Linh James, an Amerasian war baby.

Howard and Barbara were the only two vegetarians on the trip, so they were assigned to the same table at meals. When touring on buses, they competed for and finally shared the spacious backseats that they both coveted. Howard is a big guy who needs to stretch out and Barbara likes to see everything going on around her.

Barbara noticed that Howard was constantly on his handheld typing away. She admonished him for working while on vacation. He told her that he was writing poetically to deal with his life. He was healing from severe losses (his best friend to ALS, his Mom to breast cancer) and his own cancer diagnosis. He said that, in dealing with his health, he had become a vegetarian, invested deeply in yoga, meditation and other forms of spirituality, and that he was using writing primarily to generate freewheeling poetry, which made him feel better. He would write poems until he reached a point of calmness.

Barbara is a longtime writers' coach for both professionals and aspiring authors and had been aware that writing to feel better fell under a category identified by both the literary and the medical/psychological communities as "bibliotherapy." Examples of this pursuit are journaling and memoir writing. She had lost two parents not that long before the trip and was herself writing family histories to preserve her parents' legacies and to also gently "let them go."

Howard's technique was fascinating to her and she asked him about his process. He said that he would take a situation that was causing him anxiety and then write poems to create a more peaceful environment. He also said that the poems were like "snapshots" and did not bind him to particular thoughts but actually freed him of them. Barbara began to experiment with this technique on her own and found that she was able to let go of fears that she had held onto for years.

Back in Los Angeles, the friendship continued and Barbara and Howard attended journaling groups and memoir writing classes together. Instructors had wisdom to impart, but writers in these groups often tended to "run off" with words or get stuck on one subject. The duo soon realized that they had a bibliotherapeutic technique to share that would help folks to "write themselves happy, healthy and whole."

In April 2018, they started "workshops" and invited folks to Barbara's home. Each workshop was structured the same way. Barbara would begin them with a meditation and then Howard would read prompts and ask the attendees to write poetically in 10-minute intervals whatever came to mind. They would then read out loud and share their writing. Their work was never critiqued. Rather, each writer always received a simple "thank you" from the group for sharing. Howard encouraged them to write "from the heart, without ego." He reminded them that ego is the annoyingly judgmental voice that hovers, emphasizing self-esteem and, worse, self-importance, and that ego induces people to purposely write for consumption and even publication—not for self-revelation.

For Memorial Day Weekend of 2018, Barbara and Howard traveled to a country home in central Massachusetts to share their process with a dozen or so people, mostly advertising creatives and branding experts. They were hosted by commercial director, the late Murray Bruce, and his wife Gail Bruce, creator of the culturally innovative website HipSilver. Barbara provided guided meditation, and Howard dispensed his provocative prompts. The group wrote freely for ten minutes at a time and then immediately read their words out loud to resounding "thank you's." What came forward was naked self-expression and truths that had participants laughing, crying, and otherwise "lighting up" with self-realization and fulfillment.

That weekend the process was branded as "ShiftPoetry" and subsequently trademarked. Our 22nd American Poet Laureate, Tracy K. Smith, in defining poetry, has characterized it as "writing without rules." ShiftPoetry inspires folks to write without rules—to *shift* to a better place. Murray Bruce added "improve your life one stanza at a time." Barbara and Howard reaffirmed that their purpose was for folks to write themselves "happy, healthy and whole."

The frequency of ShiftPoetry sessions increased and spread to New York City and State and several locations in California, from Los Angeles to San Francisco. The process was presented internationally in Wellington, New Zealand, and Hydra, Greece.

Howard and Barbara had planned to write a "ShiftPoetry manual and workbook" but first, with Barbara's encouragement, Howard needed to complete a memoir titled *Walking With Kerry*, about his dear friend who lost his life to ALS, while showing Howard how to gracefully handle his own "dis-ease." Howard considers Kerry Ryan, his dog walking partner in the Pacific Palisades bluffs, to be his guardian angel to this day. Barbara was busy with her own work, but soon it became time to define ShiftPoetry on paper for people who could not readily attend workshops.

In early March, 2020, after an exquisite ShiftPoetry session at the magical OHM CENTER on the upper East Side of Manhattan, Howard and Barbara returned to Los Angeles ready to write. On March 11th, the same day that the World Health Organization directed folks to stay home so as not to contract or spread the newly acknowledged Coronavirus, both Barbara and Howard fell ill.

Diagnosed with COVID-19, even though the two were quarantined and curtailed, they were present enough to continue ShiftPoetry sessions on the internet. Their very first virtual ShiftPoetry workshop was sponsored on Zoom by the Open Temple in Venice, California. Created by Rabbi Lori Shapiro and her magical team, the Open Temple is a progressive center of worship known for "re-invigorating Judaism." The session was presented as part of a Zoom Shabbat Service and offered as a tool to help the congregation cope with the new world we were all about to experience.

Subsequent ShiftPoetry Zoom sessions became frequent and very well attended. Howard continued to dispense his varied prompts, but no matter the subject, participants always brought their writing back to the growing outbreak of disease.

ShiftPoetry's first book

During this period, Pandemic poems abounded. Realizing the trend, Howard and Barbara decided to cluster many of these poems into their first book, *ShiftPoetry in the Time of COVID-19, An Anthology of Healing Poems and a Workbook to Help You Write Yourself Well.*

Published on May 5th, 2020, it is Volume One in a planned series of ShiftPoetry publications.

The book takes a workbook approach, consisting of 28 prompts, each followed by a blank page encouraging the reader to write on the spot. There are 75 poems written in workshops by nearly 30 authors, illustrating how the prompts were used to inspire writing.

These poems ranged from the super sad yet hopeful "Just One More Hug" by a woman unable to touch her severely ailing mother, to the querulous "Amusing and Confusing" attempting to clarify a sudden new world we were forced to experience. Poems offered antidotes to quarantine, like "Isolating with Friends" and "My Isolation Fix" about chocolate!! There were defiant statements about what the world would look like once the Coronavirus lifted, including "And You Will Never Tell Me Where to Pee" an LGBTQ anthem, as well as "Flowers," a utopian post COVID-19 imagining. "None of Us Is Immune" pondered the near death of a strapping young man. "Coping" and "Grateful" helped both the authors and their readers to forge a path to understanding, acceptance and even hopefulness in the face of this still growing pandemic.

The book opened with a deeply emotional poem "The Man in the Bed" by Howard Kern—a tribute to ShiftPoet Jeffrey Hollander's brother needlessly taken by the virus. It ended with Barbara Ligeti's aspirational, future thinking "Wrap Your Troubles in Dreams, and Write Your Troubles Away" a directive for ShiftPoets.

ShiftPoetry in the Time of COVID-19 succeeded in setting forth a unique and effective system of bibliotherapy which has become habit forming for many, and lifesaving for more than a few.

ShiftPoetry Contributors

Although their poems also appear in their books, Howard and Barbara are dedicated to being inclusive. They are dedicated to "democratizing writing poetry." They believe that anyone can write. Emulating a well-known and successful Nike campaign to sell running shoes and encourage people to exercise "if you can walk you can run," the team declares "if you can talk, you can write."

ShiftPoetry maintains that "whatever you write is perfect" as long as it is written from the heart. In sessions, both in person and on Zoom, Barbara sits in front of a sampler given to her by her sister, Lydia. It states: "What happens at Grandma's stays at Grandma's." ShiftPoetry workshops offer the same kind of intimacy and confidentiality featured in 12 step meetings and group therapy sessions.

Among ShiftPoets there are some professional writers, but they are encouraged to drop the professional persona and just open their hearts and write. An 11-year-old ShiftPoet (Barbara's granddaughter Lucy) nailed it; she observed that ShiftPoetry encourages "writing for heart not art." She added that it is okay to take one's work public, even to publication, but that isn't the objective of the practice!

ShiftPoets are a cross-section of individuals, including teachers, parents and grandparents, Generation Zers, lawyers, accountants and financial advisors, advanced yoga and meditation instructors, and even a first responder nurse who is also expert in Chinese medicine.

A number of psychotherapists and other mental health professionals are regulars in ShiftPoetry workshops. Their response affirms that this technique is a healthy extension of therapy—giving a person tools to work on issues between therapy sessions. ShiftPoetry is a safe way to relieve stress and other conditions.

ShiftPoetry's latest book

Poetry Without Pants: Written When Nobody's Looking is Volume Two, the second book in the ShiftPoetry series.

As the pandemic created a "way of life" all of us are still sorting out, ShiftPoets attempted to return to varied familiar subject matter in their writing. Aside from offering "general sessions" with a broad selection of topics, there were special interest workshops set up (examples: "Honoring the Life of Ruth Bader Ginsburg" and "Celebrating Breast Cancer Awareness Month"). However, many poems still hovered around the subject of COVID-19, but in a different way than before.

In this volume, many poets set aside torrents of feelings and started to write about specifics of staying inside, social distancing, mask wearing, and even the hilarious subject of Zoom wardrobes. Some of the writing is still quite serious, addressing such topics as growing youthful nihilism. Other works offer lighthearted reflections, pondering the perfect choice of pandemic pod members and naughty behavior behind closed doors. Still others address exploration of new hobbies, new habits, relationships cemented, broken or reconfigured during this strange time, and much more.

There are poems that were directly prompt driven. Then there are those that were written as individuals were developing a lifestyle of introspective writing on varied subjects. A new category manifested itself spawning works that were over the top—crazy and zany. Whether the poems were prompt driven, full practice driven, or no holds barred creative flourishes, Barbara and Howard are confident that you'll find your own inspiration—and perhaps a few laughs—in this, their latest endeavor to bring the joy of ShiftPoetry to as many people as possible.

EDITOR'S NOTE

We are excited that you are interested in opening your heart, honestly articulating your feelings, and improving your life through words. We hope to be supportive in your quest to express yourself for your own personal good and well-being.

Please visit our website, **www.ShiftPoetry.com**, to learn more about our work and to acquire our books and experience our workshops.

Since our focus is offering prompt driven writing in community, purchasing our books includes free-of-charge invitations to workshops and other activities. We also offer corporate and other group presentations of ShiftPoetry and love working with diverse sectors. We have a not-for-profit division and offer underwritten workshops when possible. We are also instituting a program to franchise the ShiftPoetry process in order to reach more people. As we grow, we will advise you of all that we offer.

For now and for always our desire is to guide folks in healing themselves the way that we have bettered our own lives through our brand of bibliotherapy. We are always accessible through our website for consultation, coaching and other forms of engagement. We want to get to know you and continue to offer our support.

Our hope is for the world to heal, for society to heal, and for each and every person to heal. If ShiftPoetry can help you to write yourself happy, healthy and whole, to improve your life one stanza at a time, we are thrilled to be your teachers, muses, readers and students.

Be well and stay safe,

Barbara Ligeti and Howard Kern

Poetry Without Pants

PART ONE:

The Workbook: Prompt-Driven Writing

Prompts, Space to Write, Poems

PROMPT #1
Zoom Wardrobe

Do you remember when it mattered what you wore?
When you may have struggled to pick out just the right wardrobe for the day,
Now many of our meetings are held over Zoom calls,
People only see us from the torso up,
This relieves us of certain concerns,
But maybe you still pick out your wardrobe based on the old normal,
Or maybe you have found ways to entertain yourself while you are on a
    Zoom call,
Think about whether there are go-to outfits that you choose for Zoom,
Focus on your choices.

When you are ready,
Begin to write poetically about the changes in your clothing choices due to
    the fact that nobody's watching.

POEMS INSPIRED BY PROMPT #1

Boxers or Briefs

Boxers or Briefs?
Tidy whiteys or a lacy thong?

It used to be a guessing game you might play in a bar.
Now the choice is made before sitting down at the computer.
Zoom call attire required only from the waist up.

I knew a woman who claimed to clean house in the nude.
Does she ever bother to get dressed anymore?
Her apartment must be spotless in this time of Covid.

It's harder for a guy.
You don't want your privates to get sucked into the vacuum cleaner.

I often wonder what my favorite female news anchors have on below the frame.
You know who you are.
Stephanie. Niccole. Katy.
Sorry Mika.

A lot of folks are spending their days in sweats and tees.
Makeup and bras optional, depending on the occasion.
But you have to wear something
Or your ass is gonna stick to the chair.

My go-to Zoom wear is a Polo shirt
And Polo boxer-briefs.
I daydream that the two Polo logos are riding off in a match against each other.
Unfortunately, they're in the hundredth chukker of this crazy quarantine.
And no one is winning.

© *Jeffrey Altshuler, October 2020, Jeffrey longs for the days when he rode real horses and wore pants*

What do I write when no one is looking?

"Poetry Without Pants" is a superb title. The truth is I am somewhat apathetic with respect to pants. Short pants. Long pants. Red pants. Blue pants. I feel like breaking into a Dr. Seuss homage in reference to pants.

Knowing that no one is looking is a compelling liberation, outdone only by the freedom of knowing no one is reading.

When I am writing when no one is looking or reading I am writing for me.

Ideas and thoughts are beautiful and the engine for all pursuit. But they can be weighty at times, while curiously also ephemeral.

The dread of the lost thought is painful. I'm thinking of two things, Thing One and Thing Two . . . it only works for Dr. Seuss. It spurs the compulsion to document – get it out of my head and onto the screen so I don't lose it.

Untethered, it is a place to unload all that you don't want others to see. Lists of fears and anxieties can populate the page.

Unlassoed, there is also room for gratitude and the silly things that brought you joy that might require a little too much explanation should others come to learn about them.

Unburdened, I feel lighter not carrying that around. I need to leave it somewhere, but there aren't many places I trust.

Unhinged, it feels like a reset button. A catharsis and a clean slate. Ready to take on more ideas and thoughts. What color did I want to make my eggs with ham?

© *Aseem Giri, October 2020, ACHiEVE Podcast Host, Father of Two Doctor Seuss Fans*
https://www.linkedin.com/in/aseem-giri-9463401/

Like Good Friends

Inside my closet they do hang
Hems gently brushing the floor
Like old friends I've not seen for a while
They await my return with patience

Without question, expectations or demands
Like good friends

Inside the tattered plaid box
A lifetime of old photographs
Memories with faded colors, curled at the edges
Taken decades ago, they await my attention

Without question, expectations or demands
Like good friends

Remember the good old days of meeting up
Sharing laughter, love, good old-fashioned cocktails
Conversations, bantering about kids, dogs, jobs
You know – life, they, too, long for my voice

Without question, expectations or demands
Like good friends

Every memory sends a message to my heart
I've not forgotten the passion we shared for
Good food, stylish haircuts
Broken in shoes and comfy clothes, they quietly await my presence

Without question, expectations or demands
Like good friends

Each unknown outside this room
Nothing here pretends to be more than it is

As life moves forward in difficult time, we often forget
Our things, drenched in awareness – years of life, begging consideration

Without question, expectations or demands
Like good friends

Genuine moments where no assumptions are made
Perhaps should remain inside the closet
Where past and future hold hands
And the present remains suspended
Like a butterfly on the air

Without question, expectations or demands
Like good friends

Do not forget, during these days of
Technological contact now replacing friendly encounters
To walk inside your closet, spend time with memories
With friends, with yourself and do not forget
Who you are or where you've been and,
Spend some time loving, being and giving of yourself

Without question, expectations or demands
Like good friends

© S.D. Fletcher, September 2020, First Responder Nurse

Zoom Wardrobe

Freedom,
no need to put on makeup,
get dressed,
or even bathe.

Ten weeks with nothing to do but walk, eat and of course, drink.
So who needed makeup?!
Lipstick an ancient memory.

Connection,
essential to the human experience.
So, we reached out.
At first, we called each other . . . maybe even FaceTimed . . .
But we needed more.

Zoom,
became the Go-to Experience.

First, socially . . .
Friday Night Beverly Hills Entourage became a Zoom drink-fest.
While I was in New York, I could still join in, as long as I was awake at 9:30pm.
But now I needed makeup, not clothes, just makeup and the proper camera angle. Once, when I was too lazy to wash my hair I added a stylish hat, prompting everyone else on Zoom to grab a hat.

Then professionally . . .
Casting Directors started doing Zoom Workshops. Okay now we're talking my potential bread and butter and I found myself quickly falling back into getting fully dressed, even bottoms on the off chance I stood up by accident and well . . .
. . . showed too much cheek!

Pants . . .
was not the issue.

Setting was . . . .

What Zoom required was not so much pants or lack thereof but scenery. What did the world see of my world and what did I want them to see? In the end, a plate on which to paint my essence!

Virtual?
Family Photos?
Blank wall?
Achievement Awards?

So a lighting package, a move to my living room, no stuffed animals on my bed or a blank wall, and makeup made the experience what it has become . . . but as I think about it . . . this is as much work as just showing up and if I were in the room I probably wouldn't worry if I had pants on.

Do I? Hmmmm

© *Pat Patterson, September 2020, "What can I say but who made these rules and why are we following them?" PatPatterson.me 310.613.1526 | View Reel | IMDb*

My Little Secret

There's something you don't know, you'd never know.
I hate shoes. Shoes hate me. I prefer to walk directly on broken glass or stones. I've done it.
The last time you saw me, everyone who saw me, thought I was taller, straighter, slimmer. I was in despair.
My toes were pinched, my arches hacked, my heels cracked. In need of repair.
Shoes are protection, power, for me they are pain.
Sprinting across the city's uneven concrete, climbing up and down the subway's tunnels, clanking across the hard wood loft.
I don't even want to wear flip flops. I despise sneakers. Flat, chunk, stock, stiletto, I sport them all and dislike them equally. Slippers included, may as well add socks to the list.
I like to feel the wood, the carpet, the grass, sand, water, pebbles, asphalt on my soles.
I want my feet on the ground, connected, free.
Now you know. And you can picture my toes.

© *Pamela Wadler, October 2020, Barefoot Executive*

Thanks To My Stylists

Wow,
This is great,
Nobody cares,
I can wear anything,
I can let my hair fly,
Nope say the Jeffreys,
You have to sit still,
What's with moving in and out of the frame?
Why don't you speak into the camera?
T-shirts will not do,
Get a haircut,
I buried my mom,
And my dad lives in another state,
But somehow their voices were channeled into two very different Jeffreys,
So I lock the chair so it doesn't move,
I have to sit up like a grown-up,
No more Tees,
Button-up or bust,
The hair is still long but is tied back in a ponytail,
I will not be bullied,
Or at least I will pretend that I will not be bullied,
And I have a microphone,
What's that?
You can't understand me when I'm reading,
But I wrote the prompts,
You're right,
I don't have to read them,
Let other people speak,
Just sit there and look pretty,
Yes Jeffreys,
Whatever you say.
So where is the freedom of being on-screen and not in person?
Nobody gets to see my choices below the window,
And Jeffreys,

You can't do anything about that,
There are benefits to not having to go to meetings,
Unfortunately,
Thanks to the Jeffreys,
They are fewer than I expected.

© *Howard Kern, October 2020, Aspiring Adult*

My Closet Is Fuller Than I Remember and My Drawers: So Many Socks!

Life used to guide me to a full laundry basket. I'd carry it overflowing down the hall the stairs and the length of the house a long flat letter z to the washing machine and sort piles of whites, lights and blues and darks and reds. And be ready for the world afresh in a few hours.

Now the comfort of clothes is assuring me smaller trips to the laundry yet more frequently.

Cool days

I'll put on something comfy and stay in it all day, maybe fall asleep in it and wonder in the morning if I can continue to wear it one more day with fresh underwear? (Though that only happened once.)

Hot days:

How little can I wear and how often can I shower?
I'd wear water as clothing.
But I'm still visible.

Zoom is part of my daily life and so are long walks in the neighborhood.
Yes everything may still be color coordinated to my sneakers or jacket . . . old habits die slowly.

Some slow days I'll rally into something lovely when I venture into the closet; taking out things that signified a party or a dinner with friends, try them on in an expansive morning, and check the full length mirror to see how my aging form looks in the bias cut flow of a long dress, marveling at the extra girth in a wrap-around from a few years back . . . perhaps I'll combine a new outfit from old friends.

I've always been amazed that it would take acquisitions from three continents to put together an outfit.

My work clothes linger waiting for more than a glance, the background is more important than what I'm wearing, I will wear a top that fits a conferenced mediation and attempt to look dignified. It must be free of stains and ragged edges, but so neutral as to disappear from attention.

I've even acquired some newer things, my thrift store fingers tamed from stroking the colorful racks to sort kinesthetically; my eye now trained to seek the gems that will abide in my over full closet. The one that has yet to transition to autumn.

For that the extra-large red suitcase comes out and the cashmere and sweaters emerge and some of the sundresses the sandals and the short skirts disappear for another six months. There have always been some southern California holdouts.

The in-between weather hovers here for what might be half the year, making this my favorite weather cycle with the longest ever autumn and spring and the shortest winter I've known.

But even here Daylight savings' end usually sent me on a plane to the lower hemisphere to wonder at the Southern Cross and embrace an emerging summer for an extra month and Asia would compel me for another.

I could pack light and be away for those months dancing in beaches and soaking tropical humidity for skin nourishment and explore countries and cultures with a refined palette of sarongs, woven tops, and swimsuits,

Everything I'd need for the weeks away with the down jacket only for the plane ride there and home. The idea of living in the land of my paternal grandmother where the sun doesn't rise for more than a glimmer all winter would need a different closet and a different incarnation of me to occur.

My thermometer is magnetized to the middle numbers and so is my wardrobe. I've loved the summer visits to the endless sun,

The long days on gorgeous lakes and walks in the northern forests when there is no need for long underwear or mufflers.

I love the feel of soft and warm on my skin,

But I'm grateful that I'm facing winter in LA, with only a few thermal layers to employ before the never-ending cycle of life without LAX returns to something more connected once more.

But I'll definitely be wearing pants.

© *Jo Cobbett, September 2020, Dance and Creative Movement Expert www.movinground.com*

Hygiene—A Thing of the Past

I walk around in my boxers all day,
Sometimes I have to take a Zoom call,
I think,
Shit,
I have to shave,
So I dust off the razor,
And trim the garden,
I open my closet door,
The pants are neatly hung,
Crisp pleats and all,
I look at the shirts and ties,
Pick out the closest ones to me,
Button up the shirt,
Fix the tie,
I look at myself in the mirror and think to myself,
I really should change these boxers,
Just not today.

© *Pig Pen, September 2020, Sloppy and Happy*

Maskinista

I am a middle-aged man, who could never grow a beard,
I have no hair on the side and not much above the chin,
COVID-19 created a monster,
I have a mask for every day of the week,
Many complained about the mask,
I embraced it,
Some days I am Captain Jack,
Other days Dr. Welby,
And when I'm feeling really crazy,
No,
That's not Cleopatra,
It's me.

© *D R Fauci, October 2020, Needing a Vacation*

Graduation In A Pandemic

When I started college four years earlier,
I had dreams of graduation,
Hearing my name being called,
And accepted my degree from the Dean,
I never would dreamed of a pandemic,
Or Zoom,
Or a virtual graduation,
But all that happened,
It made one choice easy,
My gown,
And nothing else,
That was my little secret until just now.

© *Class of 2020, September 2020, Happy There Are No Breezes*

Please, can't we just have a phone call?

Childhood Disneyland memory:
Pavillion in Tomorrowland. Future phone exhibit.
You in one room, your friend in another.
Pick up the receiver. Magic.
Not just a disembodied voice
but a screen showing your friend
talking to you via video call.
How cool!! Wonder if we'll get this in our lifetime?

Flash forward. Today.
No! Not another video call.
Do I have food in my teeth?
Anything weird in the background?
Ugh. My hair sucks.
Is that ketchup on my shirt?
Oh, no. Have to sneeze.
No, not sick. Really—thanks.
Shit—husband just started
singing Sinatra in the shower.
Press mute. Camera off.
"Honey—please! I'm on a call!"
Sound on. Camera on.

Crap. He didn't hear me.
He's walking in here.
Dripping wet. No towel.
"What did you say?"

How many times do you
have to click "Leave Meeting"
before you actually do?

© *Kat Georges, October 2020, threeroomspress.com*

PROMPT #2
Alone

We have had less time with other people for the past several months,
We also have had more alone time,
Or time with our pod,
During this period,
What have you done differently than before?
How have you entertained yourself when nobody is looking?
Think about different ways you have made your life more tolerable during these very strange times.

When you are ready,
Begin to write poetically about how you have entertained yourself when you are alone during this pandemic.

POEMS INSPIRED BY PROMPT #2

Same Old Same Old

With coffee brewing in the morning,
with no one looking I load a bowl,
grab my iPad and start to scroll.

The news is the same as it was before
Black men dying more than ever before.

After my read I grab my gloves and mount my concept one
Ten thousand meters is the goal in 30 minutes or so . . .

After I'm done I call my friend of 50 years,
and then we talk about what happened again.

After an hour I situate myself in a comfy chair with all of my books . . .
No one is looking so I have another bowl . . .

I grab a book that happens to be Kant
And I follow the bread crumbs that lead me to Sartre.

© *Kermit Pace, October 2020, Educator, Athlete, Activist*

Back and Forth

I need to move.
I have to move.
The stress is palpable.
It's a bit too cold to go outside.
And the virus is outside, beyond the front door.
So I stay safe in my space.
And I walk.
Phone in hand tracking each stride
Back and Forth
Step by Step

Calls from friends
Walk and Talk
Talk and Walk
Back and Forth
Pick up the pace
Kick up the heart rate
Lower the stress
Step by Step
The steps add up
One Mile
One and a half miles
Two Miles
Gosh, I sure hope I'm not driving the neighbors below me insane.

© *Jeffrey Hollander, October 2020, Social Influencer*

Alone is Fine with a Good Bottle of Wine

Thoroughly enjoy taking trips to the wine shop
I often take the long way as I need the extra two blocks for clarity . . .
Wearing mixed match socks, basketball shorts, and a floral fleece—
    I truly feel at peace . . .
Peace because I am alone in a mask
No one can judge me, no one can see me
It's quite satisfying . . .
The wine shop is my home away from home
$120 later I feel like my missions are accomplished
I know I have something to look forward too when I arrive back to
    my natural habitat

© *Dorian Braxton, October 2020, Publicist, Avid Wine Consumer & Fashion Enthusiast*

Enjoying Quiet Time

What do I do when no one is looking?
Nothing at all.
It's the one thing you can rarely do with others.
You don't have to entertain.
No conversation.
No action.
No noise.
No worries.
Just stillness.
Me and my thoughts.
And sometimes, pizza.

© *Nicole Abunassar, October 2020, Traveler & Aspiring Digital Nomad*

Alone Time

What do I do when no one is watching?
Rearranging things in my house,
My clothes are often lost in transition,
Chasing Charlie around the house,
Watching massive amounts of Drag Race
While piling on more and more mascara

© *Emily Sims, September 2020, Scorpio & Sarcasm Enthusiast*

Thank You Netflix

I am addicted to TV,
Have been my whole life,
From the early Superman episodes to This Is Us,
This has been my life,
The hardest time for me was always the summer,
I hate reruns,
My daughter can watch the same show over and over again,
And never tire of it,
Not me,

One and done,
And my favorite time of year was the fall,
When new shows were launched,
And old series would pick up from their season's cliff hangers,
I was a weird child,
I hated the summer and loved the fall,
But I guess it's because I enjoy people,
This fall is different,
No new shows,
Weird NBA finals,
I have not even turned the channel from a baseball game,
It's like it has been one long summer,
But the things that have helped me get through these times are the angels of my Universe,
The streaming services,
Netflix,
Hulu,
Amazon Prime,
Sometimes HBO,
I have watched more bad movies,
And more sappy series than I have ever watched in my entire lifetime.
I have given new meaning to binge watching,
In Back to the Future,
Michael J. Fox says to his past self,
There are 500 channels and there's still nothing to watch,
It's still true,
But at least I can pretend,
And dream of future episodes of my favorite dramedies,
Or maybe I will write my own,
After all,
We all have been living one.

© *Howard Kern, October 2020, Streaming Video Advocate*

Who Needs Razors?

I dreaded the lock-down,
No more office,
No dishing with the girls,
Just me and my cat,
I remember how I dreaded it at first,
And then after a week of no shaving,
I thought to myself,
This isn't so bad.

© *The Girl in Pants, September 2020, Advocate for French Style Everywhere*

The New AIDS

I'm a gay man,
I have been my whole life,
I read about many men like me, who died in the 80s,
I escaped that plague,
I was lucky,
I'm not taking any chances this time,
I buried my brother, who died of COVID-19,
No human contact until I feel safe,
In the interim,
I have become a social influencer,
My friends think I'm silly for commenting on celebrity websites like a teenage girl,
But I like following 20-year old hunks,
I'd like to blame it on COVID-19,
But it may just be me.

© *Honest Joe, September 2020, Isolated but Still Breathing*

The New Gym

Pre-COVID-19,
I belonged to gyms,
Yoga studios,
I had trainers,

My paycheck was shared between me and the wellness industry,
Everything's different now,
My living room is my gym,
I take three yoga classes a week,
I have a trainer on my Android that I work with four days a week,
I am in better shape now than ever,
So what have I done to entertain myself in this time?
I model my fitness attire,
I figure,
I'm in great shape,
I might as well look good,
Even if I'm the only one who's looking.

© *Jack La La Lane, September 2020, Alone and Looking Good*

Nothing Different For Me

I'm retired,
Have been for years,
So not seeing anyone is not new to me,
What is new is how many people can relate to my life now.

© *Retired American, September 2020, Welcome to the Club*

My House Has Never Been Cleaner

I watched all the movies I was interested in on Hulu, Amazon, and Netflix,
I binged on the TV shows,
So what next?
I channeled my mom,
And cleaned my house,
Looking good,
Still nothing to do,
So I cleaned some more,
Mom would be proud,
I need a massage.

© *Hazel Baxter, September, 2020, Cleaning is Contagious*

PROMPT #3
Time with Your Pod

Even though we have not been able to see most people,
There still are people that are within our respective bubbles,
Think about how you have been spending your time with these people,
What interesting games have you come up with?
When we were children,
We played,
Have you been able to "adult play" during these days of isolation?
Have you become closer to different people within your pod?

When you are ready,
Begin to write poetically about your adventures with your bubble people during COVID-19.

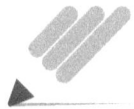

POEMS INSPIRED BY PROMPT #3

Enjoying Mom Time

Spanish series
Watched in three days' time
Watched with my mom
Watched without her
Didn't tell her
Made her think it was my first time watching it
Put my acting skills to test, like the actors in the Spanish series
Immersed in this Spanish series
Created fake fan theories, created lies
Like the actors in the Spanish series

©*Esmeralda Garcia, September 2020, Publicist & Neflix Addict*

Photos Anyone

I was never one for selfies,
I always was the one behind the camera,
I also was with the people that I wanted to be with,
When I wanted to be with them,
But it's different now,
I can't see people all the time,
I do talk to some people much more often,
Some people I have lost touch with,
But I have learned the power and magic of selfies,
For a period of time I took selfies every day,
And shared them with a special person,
Who was distanced from me,
We made up stories behind the selfies,
And created different personas,
I discovered my inner ham,
Which was absurd on multiple fronts,
First off,
I'm Jewish and ham is traif,
But also,

More importantly,
I'm a vegetarian,
And ham is traif,
But I did fall in love with the camera,
Or at least my alter-ego did,
And you can say I was phishing for compliments,
Which my friend generously provided me with,
I don't think that I will see bright lights or red carpets in my future,
But it has been fun,
Pretending,
Being someone else,
Fantasizing,
Having fun,
Tasting the forbidden fruit,
And not throwing up,
The other thing that has enabled me to enjoy selfies is my motto,
"Let Go Ego,"
That may sound like something that would prevent me from engaging in a selfie smorgasbord,
But you'd be wrong,
If you ever saw my photos,
Which you hopefully never will,
You'd see that if I had an ego,
I would find a much better model for the photos,
But with Coronavirus in the air,
I guess I will have to do.

© *Howard Kern, October 2020, Selfie Expert*

I Never Knew How Much I Would Miss Chucky Cheese

I am an older dad,
Entertaining my young child during normal times is hard enough,
But doing so during this Pandemic has required a Herculean effort,
500 stations and nothing to watch on TV,
I can only play the same video so many times,
Even five year olds get bored,
My back is aching from all the pony rides,
We can't play the games I played as a kid because they are not PC,
I'm exhausted,
Some days I feel like if the Pandemic doesn't get me,
Parenting will,
Chucky Cheese,
Help.

© Raul McDonald, September 2020, Hamburguesa Gourmet

The Year Without A Summer

Every year my children and I have looked forward to the same thing,
Summer camp,
The ultimate reprieve for moms everywhere,
No rushes to get the kids out,
No homework,
Yay,
Time off after nine months,
But not this year,
Some camps were open,
But I couldn't do it,
I was too afraid to trust Uncle Buck to properly protect my kids,
So this year,
Camp Mom,
Yay me,
At least somebody is happy.

©*June Cleaver, September, 2020, Tired but Still Smiling*

Now I get it

Being a dog,
I have little to complain about,
I bark mostly for fun,
My master is big and doesn't need protection,
But this pandemic is tiring,
When we go on walks,
I can't say "hi" to anyone,
We cross the street,
No more playdates at the house,
It makes me want to growl,
All I do is chase the cat around the house,
At least I'm getting my laps in.

© Lassie, September 2020, "Hi Timmy"

Life's A Beach

I live on the Beach,
That used to assure me lots of privacy,
Not any more,
The beach is one of the few places where everyone feels safe,
I miss my privacy,
But I found a new hobby,
I yell at people who have dogs on the Beach,
It doesn't make me proud,
But I sure am happy.

© Crabby Beach Guy, September 2020, No Longer Alone

My Lover Entertains Me

I live by myself,

I have a dear friend, who I don't see often enough,

For the first few months my friend would send me photos modeling different outfits,

It was crazy,

But crazy isn't always bad,

Especially during a pandemic,

I can't wait to see my next photos,

I'd share them with you,

But I follow Dr. Fauci to the letter,

I don't leave my bubble.

© *Juliet Capulet, September 2020, Don't Drink the Kool-Aid*

My Poor Dog

I would like to blame it on COVID-19,

Surely I would not do this during normal times,

But I do get bored,

And pink is my favorite color,

I would do it to myself,

But there are Zoom calls to consider,

Poor Fritz,

I'm sure he's not the only pink German Shepherd.

© *Lady FiFi, October 2020, "Has Anyone Seen My Dog?"*

Pandemic Couple's Nights

Before the Pandemic,
Going out with couples was an event,
It meant possibly driving together,
Sharing a meal,
Sometimes arguing over the check,
Saying goodnight,
And returning home,
Now couple's nights are so much easier,
Turn on the computer,
Chat for a bit,
And power off,
It's the ultimate reality TV experience,
Lucky US.

© *Getting Lazy, September 2020, Pants are for Fools*

Yoga Anyone

I was fanatical about yoga pre-COVID-19,
That changed when the studio closed,
I put my mat in the closet and took out my running shoes,
However yoga returned with a vengeance,
Flow classes Tuesdays and Thursdays,
Restorative on Monday and Thursdays,
And my favorite,
Kundalini on Fridays,
Who says life has to stop with a lock-down?

© John Zen, September 2020, "Shanti Y'All"

Zoom Isn't the Only Option But...

My sister has been the best organizer of family events during the pandemic,
But she chooses not to be a lemming when it comes to video calls,
Everyone else seems to be wed to Zoom,
Not my sister,
We have tried Blue Jeans,
Which I previously thought were pants,
Which still look better on me than in video,
And then she introduced me to Google meeting,
Which gave me and everyone on it a headache,
It went from person to person in nanoseconds,
Like Trump,
It was totally disruptive,
Last but not least was Game Night,
Which should have been named Scream Night,
Because that's what I felt like doing,
My sister has good intentions,
Just lousy choices when it comes to videoconferencing.

©️ *Jan Brady, September 2020, "Marcia, Marcia, Marcia"*

PROMPT #4
Self Reflections

Alone time can be scary,
But it also can be a time for meditation and introspection,
We probably have had enough alone time for a lifetime recently,
But hopefully we have grown from this experience,
What thoughts have gone through your mind over the past year?
Have you made any life-changing decisions based on these reflections?
How have your relationships changed?
Are you closer to some people?
Have you ended other relationships?
Are you the same person now that you were pre-COVID-19?

When you are ready,
Begin to write poetically about some of the insights that have been
    unearthed via quarantine.

POEMS INSPIRED BY PROMPT #4

Quarantine

The city's sad this time around,
The state's aflame,
Tourism's down,
I check the sidewalk to find a treasure,
There are only cigarette butts,
Sad and brown.

I take an evening walk for pleasure,
I'm imprisoned by the city's measures,
I don't get those who claim "It's not real, though,"
Then why for a year's half have I been tethered?

This entity surrounds me,
It mocks me so,
It could kill me without a sword or bow,
Those who don't fear it should take a bow,
Before they give us a jolly good show.

"It's all planned;"
You know how?
Economic struggles we're left to plow,
I was tired six months ago,
I'm more tired now,
I was tired six months ago,
I'm more tired now.

© *Ava Kitt, September 2020, A "Gen Z Member"*

I Miss

I miss the night before
A night of frantic packing
And deciding what to take
Designing the first day while I'm on the plane
Or while I'm driving up the mountain
Finally getting there
Unpacking
Waiting

Meeting each person
Falling for each one
One at a time
As we start to become a group

The feel of an unfamiliar, usually uncomfortable, bed
My head filled with thoughts of each person
As I begin to understand them
How they learn
And what they need
Those priorities pushing away any thoughts of myself
Except for how to find a good cup of coffee the next morning

I wake up
Way before anyone else
These are my only moments of quiet
Except for
The "let's all close our eyes" kind of quiet

The joy of looking into the room
And seeing people actually giving Thai Massages

Jousting with the inevitable nervous student
Who can't help but ask a million questions

And the fun of seeing them finally let go
And focus on the other person
On the moving energy
On the moment

I miss the intoxicating smell of food
Made from scratch
And created to support us

The deep two-hour afternoon rejuvenating nap
The hugs
The tears
The deep places people can go
The close presence of being next to people

© *Phoebe Diftler, September 2020, 21st Century Sensai*

Enjoying Family

In a weird way not much has changed.
I'm never alone so always have to have clothes on
I am a creature of habit so
Morning rituals do not change
I might wear cargo shorts with my dress shirt
But I haven't gone full Lebowski
I wish I could but I'm never alone
Which may be a good thing
I'd go crazy but not like Prince
Dirty and smelly and a little sad
But I've got people to impress
Or at least judging me
And my son is a home body
Mornings with Dad? Playdates with Grandma
He's outside with her right now
So I am never alone
And I am very lucky

© Patrick Durkin, October 2020, Awesome Dad of Traigh James

Finding Me

Off camera is when you're truly yourself, right?
Yet, during these interesting times I tend to find humor in myself when I'm being silly and experimenting with my identity
Humor is my party favor – it can hide my insecurities but also shine a light on my strengths
I never minded being on camera, but during this year I have realized I am more a creature of comfort
Finding that in both my daily routine, wardrobe, & how I present myself
Without the old routine pre-covid, I used to have to branch out more with different opportunities
I found I am happy with what I am comfortable with but do not fear what the future can manifest itself to be
As long as I stick to my roots & be the best version of me

© *Casey Keshner, October 2020, Curious Soul & Adventure Seeker*

Morning Thoughts

It's 10 in the morning,
I wake up,
Put on the fresh air
And morning breeze
As if
They are my clothes
As none of us'll need
Any of those

© *Tara Liao, October 2020, Pisces & Boba Connoisseur*

Hello Goodbye

Hello new friend,
It's really happening,
It took a pandemic to bring us together,
But it's really happening,
Goodbye old friend,
We had quite a ride,
Sometimes it was fun,
Like riding space mountain,
Other times it was monotonous,
Like riding the little cars around the track,
The kids loved it,
But we were not kids,
We tolerated it,
We thought that it was as good as it would get,
But we were wrong,
It wasn't good,
It wasn't good for a while,
I realized it first,
But then you saw the light,
I have a new friend as do you,
It's hard saying goodbye,
But it is even harder waking up to a lie,
COVID-19 did not kill me,
It did remind me though that life is fragile,
And every moment is precious,
So why waste it drinking Diet Coke,
When Dom Perignon is offered to you,
I am not the same person I was back in February,
Nor am I the same person as I was when I started writing these words,
Time doesn't stop,
Change is inevitable,
Hello new friend,
Goodbye old me,

Cheers to good times,
May every day create beautiful memories,
So new friend,
Fasten your seatbelt,
We are about to enter Space Mountain.

© *Captain Jack, October 2020, Novice Space Traveler*

Filling Holes

There's a bike lane on Westwood Boulevard, so kind of them, right?

A whole 18 inches of pavement and a white strip—which from the looks of it, was painted by a slightly drunk high school football coach—separating us from the heavy machinery to our left.

Anyway, I ride this route a few times a week because a few of my more-hip pals live in Palms.

It's all fun and games until I hit National, you know, with the Trader Joe's on the corner?

There, right after the intersection on a slight uphill, is a hole in the middle of the street.

I forget about it every time and have approximately 0.2 seconds to decide whether to fall left into the Trader Joe's parking lot (for what it's worth, I'm sure they'd immediately offer to pay my medical bills and send me on my way with a frozen dinner), or tip into oncoming traffic.

It's a gamble every time.

So I think I've had it.

I'm going to file a maintenance complaint with the city.

No one can stop me.

This hole in the ground is a tangible project, a real life place on the corner of Westwood and National, where I can bury all the things I can't deal with right now—the possibility of impending political doom, looming student loans, being. inside. all. the. time, the fact that I'll never write like Jeffrey Gettleman or sing like Adrianna Lenker, wondering why the new Bruce Springsteen album made me cry (it shouldn't have), being hesitant of celebrating a new decade for both of my parents, never remembering the difference between the French dessus and dessous, state led violence at home and abroad, and everything else—and covering them in asphalt.

© *Alexandra Weber, September 2020, Activist and Cyclist*

Dating During a Pandemic

I have been married for three decades and have suffered through my spouse's indiscretions,
I finally said enough is enough,
I signed up for online dating services to meet Mr. Right,
Not the best time,
But given social distancing and masks,
At least he won't be Mr. Right now.

© *Norma Rae, September 2020, Single and Hopeful*

What's It Like to Wear a Skirt

I am so bored,
Business is slow,
I'm on the public dole,
I wander round the house,
And take a gander at my wife's blouse,
I open her closet door,
And spy a skirt draped on the floor,
In my mind I do devise,
The skirt will be this quarantine's prize,
So I strip down to my naked bod,
Tuck away my jutting rod,
I step my legs into the skirt,
My brain goes on red alert,
I wonder if I've gone too far,
I think that all that's missing is a bra,
I clasp the bra behind my back,
Makeup I still do lack,
I peruse the stash for some blush,
No one's here,
There is no rush,
Pink will do upon my face,
I find a blouse of fancy lace,
COVID-19 has impacted me,
Oh darn,
I have to pee.

© *Rude Paul, August 2020, "Can someone help me with this zipper?"*

Mani-Pedis Aren't For Everyone

I miss my salon,
Sitting in the chair with my head back,
Feeling like a princess,
I wish I could do my own nails,
But that doesn't work,
So one day,
I'm feeling particularly bored,
My dog at my side,
Poor baby,
I guess pink is just not her color,
I wonder where my cat is.

© *Momma Kass, September 2020, Missing Cat*

Rediscovering Family

Before the COVID-19 lockdown,
I thought I knew my family,
However after seven months of living in my childhood home with my sister and
    my newly retired parents,
I know them now better than ever,
And three letters come to mind,
TMI.

© *Elroy Jetson, September 2020, "Beam Me Anywhere Scottie"*

Poetry Without Pants

PART TWO:

Writing When Nobody's Looking

Highlighted ShiftPoets

JEFFREY ALTSHULER

"Looking out from my desk, it's like a scene from Hitchcock's Rear Window. *Sometimes I think we're all living in one of his films. Oh, to be able to go out to the movies again."*

Jeffrey is a man of words, although poetry was not his chosen weapon. Writer, producer and director in film and theatre, he has been a journalist, editor, and magazine publisher. He also has a background in marketing. In addition to being a regular in our East Coast Workshops, Jeffrey is one of the ShiftPoetry insiders. He made significant contributions to our first book, *ShiftPoetry in the Time of COVID-19*, and came up with the title and shaped the format of this book. ShiftPoetry is grateful for all the selfless contributions Jeffrey has made.

Ode to Mitch and the Sun King

At first, he didn't think Trump could win the Primary.
So he could be critical.
Almost patriotic.

Then he didn't think Trump would win the election.
So he had to keep his powder dry.

Then Trump won.
And Mitch McConnell became President.

The Sun King.
Glowing orange,
Feckless, clueless and narcissistic.
A useful idiot.
A wannabe dictator.
Never more than a shill for his eponymous clothing brand,
The emperor has no clothes.

The other,
His Richelieu.
Perpetually scowling through the halls of the Senate.
A Machiavellian opportunist
Concerned only with his own perverse agenda.

Sitting around in my underwear,
Cable news my only companion,
Dickens comes to mind:

"It was the best of times.
It was the worst of times . . .
It was the season of light.
It was the season of darkness . . .
It was the spring of hope.

It was the winter of despair . . . "

Six months into the Pandemic,
The most crucial election of our times on the horizon,
I wonder . . .
Will I ever put my pants on again?

Iceberg 2

Over and over,
Politicians pontificate –
"The times are dire,
We need all hands on deck."
They say.

But we are on the Titanic.
And Leo and Kate are nowhere to be found.
Probably self-isolating.
As Lysol cocktails are passed around.

The crew shouts
ICEBERG AHEAD!
While the band plays
HAPPY DAYS ARE HERE AGAIN

The politicians rush for the lifeboats.
Pushing away the old folks,
Too weak to swim.
Unable to float.

And as the ship begins to sink,
The Captain leads the band.

Proclaiming that there's nothing to fear.
The iceberg is melting,
And we will soon reach land.

The Captain, it seems,
Suddenly believes that
Climate change is real.

Wildcat '63

Car shopping with my dad.
Not yet old enough to drive,
Still, it catches my eye.

Crimson red
With a black vinyl top.
Two doors.
Bucket seats.
Chrome side panels.
Spoked hubs.
Three hundred sixty horses under the hood.
Its power is instantly understood.

The Nineteen Sixty-three Buick Wildcat.
A teenage boy's second-best wet dream.
Who wouldn't want a car like that?

Wrecked my knee.
About to have surgery.
No sports.
No girls.

Not happy.

Operation's over.
Leg in a cast.
Long before perc and oxy.
The doctor says the pain won't last.

Dad shows up.
A sly smile on his face.
He hands me my crutches
And points out to space.

In a rare teenage moment,
I decide to obey.
What the hell,
It's a sunny day.

So I get to my feet.
Then looking outside,
My eyes and dreams meet.
That crimson red Wildcat is parked in the street.

Someday, that car will be mine.

Thank You, Jess

When I first saw you,
Held you in my arms,
You filled my heart with feelings I had never known.
A purpose beyond myself.
I knew
You were meant to be my daughter.
I knew
There was a God.

Your curiosity.
Always probing.
Always asking . . .
Why?
Asking now,
When and how?

I have no answers.
No solutions.
Only hope that
Our long talks never end.

Thank you, Jess
For still giving me purpose.
For giving my life meaning
Amidst the confusion.
In spite of the separation.

PHOEBE DIFTLER

"I was asked what ShiftPoetry has done for me? I've always expressed my creativity visually; it is how I experience the world. I ultimately went to Parsons and became a Graphic Designer and a Creative Director. When I designed magazines, I worked with writers and I saw us as having distinctly different skills. So, I was really surprised to find that I can actually write poems that I love, like I would love a drawing or a design I created. Also, for the past two decades I've spent a lot of time in groups, as a student and ultimately teaching. So, during this strange time of physical distancing, having a ShiftPoetry group to connect with and a chance to express myself and also hear about how other people are journeying through this time has kept me going."

Phoebe is a yoga instructor and a Thai massage therapist. Her focus on life has always been to help others grow and feel better. During COVID-19, she has been hosting weekly Zoom restorative yoga classes and has a growing following. She definitely is one of the people that have stepped up to make other people's lives better during these difficult times.

The Butterfly

The Butterfly breathes
She stretches magnificently patterned wings out
And flies

Seeking without trying
Seeing without looking
She is drawn to her equal
Without effort
Feeling exhilarated as she merges with him
Free of the usual caveats
And imposed boundaries

She exhales deep
And feels herself expanding
She begins to soar

She looks down at her past
And lessons learned
From being on her own

She catches a glimpse of the future
Gorgeous and lush
Intimate and connected

She is ready to live big

You Are Striped

You are striped
With leather buttons
Created by Betsy Johnson herself
I found you at a store in Tennessee
A miracle at the time
For sure

You had long sleeves
And flared out at your bottom
Like an A-line dress

I've been thinking about you lately
Trying to find you
Or at least one of your identical twin sisters

I made the choice a long time ago
To give you up
Because you sagged
And didn't flare out anymore
I regret that to this day

But we had our time together
And it was divine
You brought great style to my early life

I even met someone who helped to create you
She was excited to hear about our connection
But she doesn't know where or if you exist anymore

Still I look

This Time

I've been working my ability to allow
To trust in a timing
Beyond my will
I'm finding a wisdom
Beyond what I think should happen

So far beyond me
That I can't reach it
I can only wait
For it to come to me

And when it does
Time has helped me
To understand it
I see that ability staying with me

And I think it's possible
That people who've lived through this time
Will savor time
In a way that people
Who lived through the depression
Save food and money
In case they run out again

You will be able to tell
We lived through it
When we say
I'm going to stay home and think today
And have a day with no agenda
Like the old days

Good Luck

A friend stayed with me during lockdown
And I loved making dinner for us every night
Sometimes I would have to go deep into the pantry to come up with something creative
One of his favorites was black eyed pea fritters
Made from cans of black eyed peas that I had planned to give to friends as New Year's gifts

I grew up in the south
And the tradition is to eat them on New Year's as part of a good luck dinner

I had big plans to wrap them up
And give them to friends
But they ended up becoming fritters

24

I heard about you
Before we ever met
You were my friend's cousin
A brilliant guitar player
And an artist

I still remember your painting of a ballerina
In black and white

You were sweet
And also mysterious
As you came around on your own schedule
So when you did
It was exciting

You left me drawings sometimes
I still have one
It says ten thousand bucks
And I loved it more than if it had been real

You were irresistible
I climbed into your bedroom window one time
Just to be near you

You were tall with shaggy hair
Your style was grunge
You looked messy
Like a luxurious unmade bed
That you long to crawl back into

You were
And then suddenly
Abruptly
Shockingly
You were not anymore

You were twenty-four

STEFANIE D. FLETCHER

*"In a life full of welcomed responsibility,
ShiftPoetry is my one true creative outlet!"*

Stefanie has been doing humanitarian work for 38 years including nursing and volunteer disaster medical work. She is now in her fourth year of Chinese Medicine School. She is married to her best friend Mark and is a proud mother of two sons and grandmother to Ava. She loves her sweet furry and feathered friends too, including three dogs, four cats, and four lovebirds.

Ode To My Pants

Every day inside my closet
You hang in longing patience
No rush inside my riposte
Await me without frustration

For now with this pandemic on hand
I reach for the classic blouse
In fear the pants won't understand
The need for shirts in this madhouse

We zoom for this and zoom for that
While waiting to be let loose
Our dreams, our whims the mental acrobats
Meant to prevent a sad recluse

Between the masks and lack of knickers
Who knows who we really are
Can't see my face or otherwise bicker
So I'll bid you a fond au revoir

I wonder sometimes how it will be
When the world gets back on track
Oh the need to be out, to be set free
To enjoy my bottoms without looking back

But for now seen only above the waist
Who knows of our underpants
We'll never be judged or slyly disgraced
Even though we never wear pants

Mis – Direction

You know the way home
As well as you know the back of your own hand
Or the hiking trails
Where you go to think and sort out life
Where the answers hide among nature's beauty
And even if you forget
Surely a rock or branch would be a saving
Reminder
Unless the path was littered with hate or
Disturbed by events you could not understand
Like at night when the darkness casts
A shadow with lifelike movements except
You know it's just a trick of the light
Much like when we misunderstand a
Message or meaning
In something new, because new means
Changing and mostly we like staying
The same
Without challenging our reality or
Our perceptions because that would cause
Distress
And our lives are built on the pursuit of comfort
Over growth
But imagine for a moment
Before you were born
The ideas of comfort or home had already been
Decided
And both were constructed in a way that meant
You were destined to be homeless and filled with pain
Because
You were born
Black
Brown
Or any color but white
Where is that path home?

Where is that comfort?
Because you see if you are not black or brown
This is akin to waking up in a foreign country
And trying to ask directions but suddenly realizing
No one speaks your language
And now imagine
You were forced to pay taxes in this new
Country
A place that told you in order to belong
You must pay for systems
Police
Education
Healthcare
Food
To support society then
Realizing every road into those systems was
Blocked
By walls, speed bumps, random barriers that
Keep you in one finite place that has no
Resources
No healthcare, no schools, no polling places to vote
Oh but plenty of police
How would you find your way out of the place delegated as
Home
But had no identifying rocks or branches because
It was decided before you were born
That you don't deserve a home, or a school or hospital
How can you begin to find the way home
When the path never even
Existed

Welcome to the America Black and Brown people live in

Every

Single

Day

George Floyd

Taken from you – the world
    Your voice
        Your presence
            Your life – so many black lives

Pulling covers tightly
Over its ugliness, raindrops falling
As the reminder, there is no more hiding
From
    This
        Truth
That we are either outraged
Or slinking back under the blanket of

White

Privilege

The glass in front of me screams
In silence, asking
To be filled with
    Righteousness
        Justice
            Action
I never had to teach my sons
A different way to behave
Around the police

Because

They

Are

White

And that glass is really screaming at me now

The cuckoo clock cockadoodledoos like a murder of crows
And oh,
Speaking of murder
    Did
        You
            Hear
Another black man in America was murdered

By the white ruling class

And nobody
Is calling
For
Understanding this time

Because that is bullshit

The crows are circling, their black beaks
Pecking
    Pecking
        Pecking

Through layers of indifference, a superficial
Veil of equality, rights only afforded
To
A
Few

The taste of shit I can't spit out
And
    Maybe
        I
            Shouldn't

Because it keeps the taste of murder awake in the
Daylight, exposed where there is nowhere to

Hide

The cupcakes baking with
That aroma of sweetness
The simplest of living
Stolen
Again

If you are not outraged
It is
Because you do not have to consider
Murder as revenge against you
Every day you wake up

And that
Is
The
Uncomplicated
Definition
Of
Privilege.

Middle of the Night

A pandemic explosion
Invisible bombs

    Cloaked in spittle
Couldn't see it coming
Except those of us who knew
Exactly what was coming
For
The
Long, long
Visit

    An uninvited guest
Planning its long vacation
Fragmented lives torn apart
Left to rot in a
Rolling
White
Morgue.

A white truck filled with
Leftovers of lives
Taken too soon
It sounds awful and feels worse
Like liquid hot lava pain
Memories lost
Families broken

No direction
On this rudderless ship
Incompetent leadership now killing us
As fast as the virus
Or
Kidnapping us

DHS unleashed on the people
Disappeared
In an unmarked rolling white morgue
Or
An unmarked rolling black morgue in Portland
Because a war is waged on the people
Being fought in a hospital
Silently
Or
In the streets, peacefully
And loudly
No running

    Or hiding
Not until we build
The inclusive
Non-violent society
Every
Human
Being
Deserves

Breach of Trust

I walked along the Earth's path, in her dire aftermath,
Looking for friends to hold and hear.
Of the suffering I see, I'll give to the trees
At this spiritual time of the year.

Don't you remember the cold in November
When the bluebird would no longer sing?
Though the wind was so chill it dared not stand still
Nor provide us with warm thermal springs.

The fog can be thick with her conjuring tricks
That play with the things we see.
Be aware of the swirls that look like pearls
They can land you on your knees.

I wish you could hear the brave Eagle's new fear
As she soars above me so high.
Her plight is unreal, we can no longer conceal
The destruction of her beautiful blue sky.

But what should we do if we dare tell the truth
about how we got right where we are?
We treat her world with disdain and dare to complain
About the cost of the fuel for our cars.

So take just a minute to truly admit it
The harm we have caused is unjust.
It's the only real way to step up and say
That we acknowledge our breach of trust.

ROBERT GALINSKY

"ShiftPoetry is one of the few sacred lifelines to my poetic muse. It allows me to go inside myself and scrape around for hidden ideas and frights, and then pleasurably forces me to express my most honest and therefore most often embarrassing of thoughts. ShiftPoetry touches the sweet, savory and sour of my soul."

Galinsky is a noted information innovator and trend identifier, in both the virtual and live space, who just signed a developmental deal for a scripted hybrid reality TV show, with *Levity Live*, and recently had a successful Off Broadway, and Hollywood, run of his one person show, *The Bench, A Homeless Love Story*.

He has coached clients for appearances on *Shark Tank*, *The View*, *ABC Nightline News*, the *Today Show*, and for multiple presentations at the United Nations. He facilitates programs to c-suite executives at Fortune 500 companies and to incarcerated youth alike, and his work as such has been featured in the *Wall Street Journal*, *New York Times*, the *Financial Times*, *Advertising Age*, on BBC, NPR and many more media outlets.

Galinsky has written/co-written over fifty TEDx Talks and is excited to be a ShiftPoet!

KOVID Haikus

rooftop oasis
swimming with the stars, upon
tar tartare terrain

desperation is
voter enthusiasm
spiraling for blocks

someone is watching
no nose picking and eating
covid reminder

sleep nap eat nap rub
lock down please don't end so soon
so good so cocoon

vote for god's sake vote
then shut the fuck up hero
post a lunch photo

adult play, threesome
double trouble in bubble,
is it worth the call?

withdrawn long ago
flawless oddities float, the
East Village bubble

New York is home, I'm
alone in strange town again.
It is Déjà vid?

big blank black onyx
backside of my eyelids, the
new cinema screens

Opening line, "I
want Covid cuddles," followed
by unfollow block

moist buttskin sticking
epidermis adhesive
brazen chairs bite back

no Covid salon?
fingernails toenails prove claws,
don't be so precious

PAM HEFFLER

"ShiftPoetry has been a joyful and deep experience for me. The sessions are supportive, sacred, and a wonderful container to explore my inner thoughts and experiences in a spontaneous way that is often surprising. It's a great vehicle for self-expression as well as being healing and transformational."

Pam is a woman of many talents, which she shares generously with the world. She is a top Pilates instructor, an actress and a dancer. Whether it is on the big screen or sitting at home with her hubby watching the TV screen, Pam always fits right in. Throughout the pandemic Pam has been busy teaching and occupying many of her clients' computer screens on Zoom. She's also been indulging in all kinds of creativity, often supported by her ShiftPoetry practice. We anxiously await the return of the highly acclaimed full length dance performance she created and performed in 2018/19 with her husband, Mark Yamor, *Train Of Love: Life And Love On And Off The Trails*, when theatres are reopened.

What Is Zoom To Me?

Since you asked what do I do during a zoom?
Mostly I participate,
I am part of,
I take notes,
Or I am sincerely engaged but when it allows I will turn of my camera.
So grateful for this option for example during a free form dance class –
Ahh the freedom,
No reason to care just dance around my tiny room or sashaying out into my living room.
What I wear depends entirely on my mood,
Something comfy for sure or creative and often mismatched
I'm definitely more carefree and only occasionally do I put something special on.
Today was one of those days.
I am part of a woman's abundance meditation group.
Our topic was luxury.
So to show up in something luxurious I put on a dress,
A silky scarf some lip gloss and eye liner just to "feel special" and celebrate just being.

All of us in our private spaces connecting over this phenomenon called Zoom.
I do hope soon,
Real soon we can be together.
Real rooms,
Real connection,
Fully clothed (perhaps still no bra!)
And we won't be so dependent on this thing called Zoom.
But until then I am grateful for our many connections in these zoom rooms!

Zoom What?

Zoom, zoom,
In my very tiny room.
Who knew?

I never really heard of zoom,
I think I only used it once before.
Technology and me – not so much.

I'd rather be outdoors,
Engaged in activity – doing, moving, creating, planning, and working.
Now all of it in front of the computer (my old PC computer).

Me and zoom are becoming fast friends.
So . . . depending on the room I'm going to zoom,
I.e. the class, group, discussion –
Dictates how I prepare.

Do I wear underwear?
I "usually" do – but for sure rarely do I wear a bra,
Because hell no one can really see if I tilt my camera up just enough,
And truth be told I don't really care if I'm in my pj's,
A sundress,
Or simple underwear –
That's what I wear.

Now I do teach so when I do I dress head to toe in my work out garb and yes a support bra (so I don't offend),
And yes a bit of make up to brighten up my face!

Oh but the hair – I have yet to cut my hair.

Snuggle Buddy

In my bubble, we like to snuggle. ugh sorry I couldn't help myself that rhyme but yes we've been spending more time me and my hubby – long walks, walking only in our neighborhood. We are the crazy couple that walk the blocks. We visit Bambi, the statue doe with her mask on, we visit the bees of Malcom and Santiago's bees which hover on his roof top and of course the Hawaiian garden and the cabin in Big Sur. We invented these places to stretch our imagination and imagine adventures that we are on. Our awareness has been heightened as we witness, the changing trees and we get to appreciate our sweet little neighborhood streets. Then there are the kitties. My husband is always in search of the cats to bring back (not really but we do get mice, so wouldn't it be nice). There seems to be a black cat visiting our backyard. Her and I, we don't like one another much perhaps it's a jealousy thing. She goes right for the man! That's ok.

Hmmm . . . new games . . . . . . not so much. Poor guy I make him tape me on my IPhone for auditions. He calls himself Steven Speilman heir director!! And of course our garden . . . How many ways to get dirty in our garden. Planting new vegetables . . . I almost forgot we sprouted seeds from our time in New York. 20 year old seeds to create our victory garden. Our blueberries exploded, we actually got tomatoes and zucchini from the 20 year old seeds.

We watch Huel Howser on PBS, Blue grass underground and *Austin City Limits*! Music music music , food and of course some wine some of the time. No real games, Just us . . . oh it's you again!! Hah . . . .no ???? No new games or Netflix or baking bread in our bubble but that's ok – like comfy shoes and a soft robe we are Happy just us in our home sweet Home . . .

|

New Discoveries – Old Memories

Mother nature is here pounding at our door and into our hearts. Time to Wake up to listen, to walk the walk not so much talk . Wake Up!!!! I used to say that to my mother who seemed to be asleep so much during my childhood. She was tired from having the twins I suppose so I would feed them when I was 2 ½.

I got so off track . . . maybe not . . . my mother and then there's Mother nature. She's crying for us to realize, to dig deep inside, to listen, to pray, to get on our hands and knees and smell the dirt to honor the earth . . . . we come from. It seems the Native Americans knew and then what did we the white folks do – rape the land, take more, more, more . . . more stuff – fill our fat tummy's up with Things. That's what we have taught the younger generation . . . Get ahead, look good, impress – Instagram and tweet – selfies about what. Watch out when we are not looking the real world is going by as we all quietly die a little more deep inside.

That is what I have come to hear, to listen, to pause, to get into child's pose – to let go – to know . . . to really know what makes my heart sing, what makes me truly come alive.

I sat in my garden for the first time in 10 years at the beginning of this pandemic. I thought. "what have we done? Why have I been asleep?" Time to wake up, to activate, to be more aware, to actually fucking really care and do something about it. Something is brewing inside, no time to hide. Get up and out, the time has come. We are not getting any younger. I ask myself what is so import, what really matters . . .

Love, nature, God or what I call Spirit, Dance, Plants, Music, Activism . . . ?

To connect, to understand, to stand in another's shoes – to look at them and say I really see You!

At the beginning of this pandemic I had a profound feeling or thought or perhaps hope, that maybe this, this will bring humanity together, for all of us in the world to come together, to heal . . . to understand, to get down on our knees and to really See . . . .

I am Waiting.

JEFFREY HOLLANDER

"I tried ShiftPoetry as a favor to my good friend, Howard Kern. I didn't think I would like it, but I was wrong. I had never written any poetry before, and now I look at the news, and I think poetically. I love ShiftPoetry and how it made a poet out of a very conservative lawyer. Thank you Howard for pushing me and introducing me to a part of me that I didn't know existed."

Jeff is a retired lawyer who spent over thirty years in the insurance business. His life, like many others, became much more encapsulated with the COVID-19 pandemic. He also has made a major shift during this time. He is now in charge of distance education and training for the ShiftPoetry team. He will spearhead a future licensing program for the company. He also heads up our LGBTQ initiative.

Why I Wear a Mask

Empathy
Selflessness
With a world view
A view of humanity
Logically
With a focus on science
With Respect for others
With Love
With simply not being an IDIOT!

Chemistry

COLD
Scientific
Test tubes
Experimental
Mixtures
Coming together
Bonding
Rare
Instantaneous
A feeling unlike any other
True love
Soulmates
HOT

Remembering Mommy

The simple things
Life's small pleasures
A moment in time
Me and my mom
My mommy
Driving in my Mercedes convertible
Top down
Sunny day
Dance version of "It's Such a Perfect Day" playing off the CD
We were just going to the mall
Nothing that special really
But
My mom had cancer
And this was a rare day when she was feeling fine
We went shopping
She bought shoes and a blouse
So ordinary
Yet so divine
I smile each time it comes to my mind.

Come Out, Come Out?

High school
Coming of age
A secret
But so much has changed….hasn't it?
New rights…yes…from the highest court in the land
But, in practice, is it really that different?
Opinions differ and people still feel it's acceptable to state them out loud
Will I be accepted?
Will I lose my friends and family?
Will I lose my home?

Will I still be loved?
At least I have some modern guides to tell me it will be okay
YouTube
TV shows and Movies, *Love, Simon, Love, Victor,* Netflix shows galore
But, reality is still there.
So I'll wait
I'll stay safe in the closet
The time will come
I do deserve a great love story
But, just not right now.

The Master Has Spoken

We, the White majority,
are telling the Black minority,
that there is no systemic racism,
even though the Black minority insist there is.

Are we, the majority,
just trying to, once again,
control and put
the minority in their place?

"You are wrong!"
"Be quiet!"
"Your opinion doesn't count!"
"We, the White Majority know better!"

The MASTER has spoken!

TWESIGYE JACKSON KAGURI

"I met Barbara Ligeti at a Hoffman Institute gathering and her introducing me to ShiftPoetry has changed my life. I am grateful to be part of such an expressive and nurturing family."

Jackson created and for the last 20 years has run Nyaka, a foundation which works with communities in Uganda to provide comprehensive care to children at risk. Many of these children were born into families ravaged by AIDS. Many are orphaned. Jackson has motivated grandmothers to be the foundation's most significant workforce. ShiftPoetry has committed to helping Nyaka with a cultural initiative to begin in 2021, to bring arts and letters from all over the world to Nyaka's children. Jackson is dedicated to his foundation work and is writing books and is available for speaking engagements through the foundation. For more please visit www.nyakaglobal.org.

Never to Come Back

It was on August 26, 1996, at 8am when you took your last breath in my hands.
I had grown up looking at you and your strength and determination.
I knew I could do anything because you were my big brother.
However, that morning, death,
HIV/AIDS, robbed us and took you away never to come back.

When your three children walked hand in hand with your wife,
I was tearing and shaking,
I knew you were gone never to come back

Our mother had travelled 13 hours to come see you before you died,
She prayed and tried to comfort us,
I looked on and did not say anything to our mom because I knew you were gone never to come back.

Seven months later, our sister who followed you died a similar death and she was gone never to come back.

Listen, you did not die in vain because I started a huge program for children and their grannies.

When I look up,
I see you and I appreciate you.
You will never come back but your spirit lives and will live forever.

This Too Shall Pass

COVID-19 came and COVID-19 will go but while it's here I agree it has changed so many things in my life.

In the past I wrote and read on planes.
This changed with COVID-19.
Since I have not been traveling,
I do not write or read at the same rate as before.
Right now, I am sleepy and thinking about quitting writing,
but I promised Barbara, so I will write.

During COVID-19, I have attended zoom calls half naked and just wearing a t-shirt.
I have gone to bed without brushing my teeth or taking a shower.
I have enjoyed my glass of wine before I sleep,
Something I did not have to do before COVID-19.
I have made friends in my bubble,
And ran short and long distances.

On October 24th, seven of us will run all 26.2 miles as part of New York's marathon virtual race.
We are running for Nyaka children and their grannies.
We have trained and checked on each other since March when COVID-19 started.
We will now be connected for all days of our lives.
Our children know each other and they will be cheering as we run mile after mile.
Thank you COVID-19, without you, this would not have been possible.

These people have become family.
We have played music, danced, cooked, baked, and relaxed in my house and their houses.
We have taken turns to test for COVID-19 so we can keep our bubble healthy and clean.
It has so far worked, no one has tested positive.
We even came up with a name "De basement Crew"
And created a WhatsApp group to stay in touch during the week and runs on Fridays.

We have celebrated birthdays and ran in honor of whoever is celebrating, 20 miles for Norman, 15 miles for my 50th birthday, 18 miles for Edith, and we will do 26.2 mile for Nyaka, the organization I started 19 years ago and oversee fulltime.

With all this happening in COVID-19, I also have a sad story that happened on March 17th, 2020.
A COVID-19 heartbreaking story.

My second marriage of 8 years ended on March 17, 2020.
You see,
I was married at 28 in 1998 and stayed married for 12 years,
I have a son Nicolas from that marriage.
In 2011, I fell in love again and re-married and have a son and twin girls from that marriage.
I wrote love stories on each marriage in my books *A School for My Village* page 43, *Victory for My Village* page 113 respectively.
Each of these marriages I convinced myself that I was ready to commit to one woman and build a long life together.
Regrettably, I cheated in both marriages, and denied, lied, and covered up my entire trauma past and present at the time.
I never looked for help to confront my demons and as a result here
I am divorced twice, alone in a home.
I have since looked and found professional help.
I have struggled more since March 2020 than I have ever struggled in my entire life.
Serving as an elder in Church, CEO of Nyaka, CNN hero, speaking at UN, publishing books, traveling the world on book tours and for keynote speeches did not heal my trauma

Now, I am on a healing journey to find a true meaning of who I am and why I exist.
To even write the word that I "cheated" is an accomplishment on my part.

One step at a time,
I truly believe there is healing.
I am not my past traumas and this too shall pass.

HOWARD KERN

"I have many poems, many of which I have not shared yet. Each of the following poems were written by me in 10-minute sprints in ShiftPoetry Workshops. When I look back at these, I am so grateful for ShiftPoetry. It not only helps me to navigate the future but also reminds me of the precious past."

Howard is a very active writer who has found that writing is the best way for him to access feelings and process emotions. As a lawyer, he has written agreements that clarify things for his clients. However, as a ShiftPoet, he has been able to clarify so much for himself. One day Howard hopes to be a functioning adult.

Boundless Joy

I am sad,
But that is a lie,
Fake news as they say,
I am happier than ever,
I have so many new and beautiful things in my life,
My children are independent,
Mostly,
I get to do what I want when I want to do it,
I write,
I run,
I play,
I walk,
I breathe,
I laugh,
I am alive and well,
I have a new business that is exciting and will hopefully bring joy and happiness
    to many,
I have great friends,
Life has never been better,
And if it has,
So what,
The past is history,
The future is a mystery,
Now is a gift,
That's why it's called the present,
So I messed that up a bit,
But you get my drift,
The possibilities for happiness and joy are limitless,
In Kundalini we say,
I am bountiful,
I am blissful,
I am beautiful,

I am all that and more,
Life is amazing and I am blessed that one sperm out of millions hooked up with one egg and created me,
That was probably the most amazing voyage of my life,
So if I could survive that,
The sky's the limit,
So stop your whining and complaining,
Do what you were meant to do,
Whatever that is,
And remember the most important rule for every day,
Smile.

Mom

We haven't spoken in years,
That's not my fault or yours,
Things happen,
People drift apart,
They change,
But that's not what's keeping us apart,
Not COVID-19 either,
Nope,
You died,
You got sick and cancer took you from us,
It deprived you of your golden years,
Your life was not yet complete,
Our time together was cut short by mutated cells,
You were a very young mom and a young grandmother,
What you lacked as a mom you made up for as a grandmother,

All your grandkids loved you,
Even other kids loved Grandma JuJu,
You were someone whom I would get into emotional battles with,
I still have some of those scars,
But you also were someone that supported me when I needed support,
I could do no wrong even if I did wrong,
You were a fierce mama when it came to your cubs,
You had an infectious smile,
You never said no to anybody,
Although sometimes you wished you had,
You overcame so many obstacles in life,
You were an inspiration even if it took your death for me to realize it,
You were not perfect,
But no one is,
We had some great times together,
I used to tease you about how you were the worst avid tennis player ever,
But you still played tennis,
And you beat people that were more skilled than you,
You never gave up,
You never allowed someone else to win,
Even in friendly games you were anything but,
Life continues but it is not nearly as much fun without you,
Memorial Day is around the corner,
I have lost many people over the years,
But you were my greatest loss,
I have multiple siblings and many friends,
But I only had one mother,
And I thank God she was you.

Baby Fritz

You were not my first pet,
There were others before you,
But you were the first pet brought home just for me,
All the other pets were for the family,
I was not as excited,
You were a GSD,
A German Shepherd Dog,
We looked for you for years,
It never worked out,
But then I found you in an ad in the Newark Star Ledger,
German Shepherd puppies,
Yay,
Finally,
Fritz No. 2 for the family,
But Fritz No. 1 for me,
I was ecstatic,
You were so small,
We took you home in a box,
You grew,
But not too big,
You were a terror,
It didn't matter,
You were MY terror,
People were afraid of you,
I loved you,
I was 13 when you came into my life,
Almost 26 when you exited,
You were MY first great dog,
It's been a long time,
Too long,
I have had many more great dogs since you,

Mirabella,
Molly,
Buttercup,
And finally Lucy,
Lucy would have terrorized you,
She also is feared when she is not revered,
I love you and miss you,
You were not my last,
But you are forever my first.

Grandma's House

It has been a while since I last visited your apartment on Surf Avenue,
I remember the cement outside,
It was in Coney Island on the other side of Seagate,
I loved to take the elevator up to your place,
Which was alive with more plants than the Amazon,
I used to wonder how you survived with so much Carbon Dioxide being produced daily,
Yours was a small place,
But I always felt comfortable,
I remember the mayonnaise eggs and pastina,
Or your fried potatoes,
There was not a lot of nutritional value,
But all your dishes were filled with TLC,
This pandemic has not kept me away from you,
It has been 28 years since you passed,
But this year is like 1992 in many ways,
We have a President who preaches hatred,
I remember you watching George HW Bush and being outraged by his language,
Language which would be mild by today's standards,
No,

The pandemic is not keeping me from you,
But it is forcing me to look deep inside,
I am lonely,
But I am also lucky,
I get to see the people that mean the most to me,
But sometimes I miss simple human contact,
I think that you came to mind because you always made me feel good,
This pandemic highlights how out of control we really are,
I miss you Grandma,
I know you suffered through rough times,
I am glad you did not have to suffer through COVID-19,
Or the more serious pandemic,
Hate.

Birthdays

I have had almost 60 birthdays during my lifetime,
Most of them just come and go,
But there are some that are more significant,
Ten was big because it was double digits,
At 13 I became a man even though my voice didn't reveal that,
20 was huge because I was no longer a teenager,
I forgot about 18,
I guess I must have been drunk,
At 25 I hit the quarter century marker,
30, 40, and 50 were the decades,
Which are always significant,
55 was cool because I was a double nickel as my dad said when he hit 55,
Then,
All of a sudden,
I am staring at 60,

It's like looking at the barrel of a shotgun,
A doctor once said that I would not make it past 60,
He wasn't my doctor,
But I still remember the conversation,
In Judaism,
It's said that you get your wings at 60,
I sometimes wonder whether I deserve my wings,
My life is looking a lot different now than it was a few years ago,
I am frightened of change,
I have resisted it my entire life,
But sometimes change is good,
What would the world be like without butterflies?
Lots of caterpillars,
I am not where I thought I would be at 60,
In all honesty,
I did not expect to be alive at 60,
But here it is,
Months away,
I have people that love me around me,
And I have people that no longer love me,
I want life to be beautiful,
I want to be a beacon for all things good,
Unfortunately sometimes I can be a pain in the butt,
But maybe once I hit 60,
I will achieve that wisdom I always sought after,
Or maybe,
I'll just chase butterflies.

GRACE KONO-WELLS

"I spend much of my time nurturing others. The ShiftPoetry workshops are a chance to get some much-needed me-time."

Grace is a woman of many talents, who shares them generously. She does important work to put food on her table, but she also focuses on making the world a better place. She has traveled overseas to help build schools. She gives freely of her time to charitable organizations. And during the pandemic, her home has become a virtual yoga studio, where she hosts at least three classes a week gratis and spreads her love and charitable spirit to her students.

Being A Leader

A neighbor, a friend, short blonde hair, brassy personality.

But that's what I love about her.

No bullshit.

She definitely has her opinions and will tell you what she thinks even if you didn't ask her to.

Be the president of the HOA, she says. You'd be great at it!

Why not you? You're bold, you're courageous, you take charge.

She says evenly that I'm nicer, kinder, more level-headed—that's what makes a good leader.

Hmm—is this a ploy to take a position where she can bend me for her own benefit?

My mind is already going there, making up stories.

Alas, I accept.

Then she reads a scathing letter she wrote to management on behalf of the HOA that is so litigious, I'm sure my mouth hit the pavement when she read it to me.

Noooo! It's not supposed to work like this.

Anger, resentment, defensiveness—walls are popping up everywhere and I am going there.

STOP! Take a breath. Don't go there.

We chat briefly. I'm hoping she sees my commitment to the community to make this place a peaceful, harmonious environment for all of us, management included.

She feels I'm weak. But . . . okay . . . whatever . . . and she leaves.

I feel unwanted, not good enough . . . as she said, "weak."

But I'm standing for the final outcome and I'm declaring a new future of happiness and harmony.

I am strong.

I am courageous.

And . . .

Fucking awesome!

Missing Mom and Hugs

I talk to my mother more often now than before. She's been gone just over a year, but I greet her every morning. She asks me how Vern is doing, and how come I don't cook for him, and why I can't be a better wife, and why I'm not a millionaire for working so hard.

My gosh—it still never ends!

And though I hear that voice, I can also hear the little four-year-old who was abandoned, whose mother died when she was two, the child who lived through the war, the girl who felt alone, unloved, who felt she had to be the best at everything to prove she was worthy. That's the woman I've grown to know, have become friends with.

We laughed at all the wild and crazy things she did in her 20s, about how shy daddy was and that she had to "initiate" things (!!!), about all kinds of things girlfriends talk about. This was before she left—but I still hear her even now. Sometimes naggy, but now more tolerant.

And I miss her so much. I wish I could touch her, look into her eyes, have tea and chat about everything and nothing.

I can never ever forever do that. And now I'm missing my friends. Plain and simple: I miss human contact. I wonder what you're thinking as you read this.

At least, once this pandemic is over, we can have some tea, chat about everything and nothing, and best of all, I can hug you.

Life in the Zoom Room

First day of a series of classes . . . on Zoom.
Okay. Fifty-eight people.
Stay on "speaker mode" they say.
But I don't.
I'm scrolling, scrolling, pausing, scrolling . . .
Do I recognize anybody?
Oh, there's Johnny! He doesn't know I'm here.
Class drones on. We do assignments. We share.
Johnny shares.
I share.
He sees me and texts me.
Glad you're here!
I send a smiley face.
He laughs—on screen—muted, of course.
In a sea of faces, I see him laughing which makes me laugh.
He texts: *Don't make me laugh!*
I laugh.
There are two *VERY* happy tiny faces in the grid view.
Stop it! I text back.
Which makes him laugh so hard, he literally falls off his chair.
Which makes me laugh so hard, I have to cover my face.
All of this silent laughter!
I can't even look at his face on the screen anymore.
I feel like we're naughty little kids in kindergarten.
. . . And it's SO FUN!
I'm trying desperately not to lock eyes with him, my face twisting into a weird line
    so as not to start laughing again.
I see other faces looking inquisitively—at me? At Johnny? Coincidence?
Apparently, they are also on grid view.
And then I discovered the "Stop Video" button.
I resume my composure and come back in.
Johnny has moved.
Awwww . . . .
And the class drones on.

Hidden Commitments

She is animated, always talking with her hands, big smiles. People say she's nice, loving, kind and patient. "A hard worker!" "You can always rely on her!"

As she walks down the street, she tosses rainbows here and there. Heart emojis seem to emanate from her very soul with sickeningly sweet Korean pop music driving every step.

She walks through the candy store, to the back room where the smell of crack baking in the dark crevices permeates the air.

She casually skips over to a table and tosses the extra rainbows on the surface. A few drop to the ground where two hermit crabs, Control and Manipulate, gobble them up.

The music has changed to something dark, ominous and royalty-free.

She sits down, puts her feet up on the table and calls for Unworthy, a small rat-like creature that whispers in her ear, "You're not good enough," every hour on the hour.

"With you, my pet," she says sweetly to Unworthy, "I'm able to control the world and make them see how wonderful I really am."

The next day, however, she forgets to feed Unworthy—something she has never done. But it was a very busy day. There was much to do! She had to care for the elderly, save the unwanted dogs, fundraise for children with cancer, lead a neighborhood community, and build schools in third world countries. After all, "She's a hard worker! She's amazing! We love her so much!"

As she toiled tirelessly throughout the day, she never once used Control and Manipulate to control and manipulate any situation she felt lost in. Normally, she ended up saying to herself, "See? I knew he couldn't do it. I have to do everything because I know how to do it right and I'm the only one who cares."

And when this happened, the world would fall at her feet and kiss her toes and hold her up on the biggest, brightest pedestal, and she would feel good again. She would feel loved. And who doesn't want to feel loved?

But today was different.

She accomplished all those things on her list and even had time for an ice cream sandwich covered with red and white sprinkles and pink sugar confetti which she never, ever allowed herself to have.

Today was different because she suddenly realized she did everything on her list because she loved doing it—not because of Unworthy. She knew in her heart she didn't need to prove anything to anybody.

And suddenly she felt free! Like she could run to the end of the street, leap into the air, and sprout wings and just fly away. She giggled at the thought.

Then she remembered she forgot to feed Unworthy.

"You know, Unworthy is kind of fat anyways. And I hope Control and Manipulate crawl away and find new homes. I know they're still part of my family, and I acknowledge them, but they're not me. Not anymore."

Then she turned up the Korean pop music, tossed a handful of rainbows in the air, and skipped down the street while REAL heart emojis emanated all around her.

BARBARA LIGETI

"ShiftPoetry has given me the most effective way yet to help people to express themselves to better their lives. Over the years, I hosted literary programs for Vietnam veterans, formerly incarcerated, the homeless, and abused women. After 9/11, I created workshops for firefighters, policemen, other first responders, and surviving family members. I am very excited to continue my work with ShiftPoetry in my toolbox. ShiftPoetry has helped me to be more open and positive about my own future as well."

Barbara has lived through both personal and public tragedies. She has learned to use ShiftPoetry to process losses. She is a strong proponent of the power of laughter and many of her poems reflect levity, and express loving memories of those she knew and lost to the Vietnam War, the AIDs pandemic, 9/11, and now this latest lingering pandemic. Barbara selected these poems, some written in response to the four prompts at the beginning of this book, generated in timed 10-minute intervals and unedited, as true examples of spontaneous ShiftPoetry.

Who Sees the Mess But Me

I've been messy of late
I've spent my whole life striving to be orderly
I come from a small nuclear family
Where cleanliness was next to godliness
My Mom prided herself on having floors one could eat off of . . .
I don't exactly get that value, but
Well, when I say I've been messy I haven't been dirty
My doggie sometimes eats off of my floors and he is just fine

But instead of putting things away after I used them, I strew them
For example, dishes get nicely rinsed but do pile up after I dine
Instead of putting things where they should be
I experiment with where they might otherwise want to live
And think of that new way
As a kind of wandering feng shui

Also if I leave a little mess at night
I've got an activity in the morning that actually generates delight

My favorite mess making activity
Is actually one that also serves my exercise proclivity
I change clothes aerobically
I've kept most of my favorite clothes throughout eternity
I once pointed out to my very grown daughter that
I can still fit into what I wore in high school
From cheerleading outfit to skinny sheath to hat
I guess nothing, not even my head, got fat

I take out books I haven't looked at in years
I re-read favorites, classics, and remember that
some literature is predictable, some in my bones
In A FAREWELL TO ARMS when Catherine is dying
Requesting of her lover that he not do anything with another

That they did together
I'm reduced to a 16 year old's ocean of tears
And when I am done with a book
Or have just had a look
At a chapter or passage I'd like to review
Then, again, I just strew

There was a time when my library was alphabetized
It will be again
Cause when the tossed salad of literature is knee high
With nothing left on shelves to espy
Re-ordering volumes will be another kind of exercise

So, what I guess I am saying is this
I am keeping my figure trim
My mind sharp
I'm being naughty in ways that I was never allowed to be
And maybe with all of this dizzy messiness
I'm finding a new me –
A little bit walled in with stuff
But actually, ultimately, quite FREE.

Bubble Buddy

Oh we were close before the pandemic
But getting together had its ups and downs
It's logistical impediments
Sometimes a frustrating headache

But Covid came and we got sick simultaneously
We were radioactive to everyone but ourselves and each other
Which caused everyone else to look at us extraneously

Being together recently, we have perfected routines,
I mean comedy acts and psycho dramas
Sometimes as if we were crotchety old folks
Sometimes as if we were just teens

We have learned how to laugh together
With, but also at, each other

Since there were no men in my life growing up
I feel like I now have a brother
Or maybe just a significant other
My brother my father
My sister my mother
My girlfriend my boyfriend
My pal and my lover
Someone to ignore me or respond to my need for a smother

Somewhere in the last seven months
I thought this whole routine had peaked
When the doorbell rang, I'd peek and sigh
And Ground Hog Day would come to mind

But then I got over that and realized
I had a new kind of relationship that would in non-pandemic times
Be very hard to find
So I cherish the consistency
The mundane and the resistancy

Is that a word?
Who cares
Cause these days everything is absurd
Like our psychobabble that others might think of as wonky when overheard

I've become precious, delicious, stimulating, silly making
Engendering and welcoming laughs and gaffs
Giggles and tears that trickle
A form of play that tickles every inch of my being
And makes me realize that with you
I am a being who is pure, honest and true

I Am Who I Am – Still

Everything is changed
Relationships have reconfigured
I've become more introspective
And have less of a tendency to be triggered

When something transpires
I have eons of time to reflect, rectify, self-conspire
Oh – and if that isn't a word – note that
If you know what it means it's in the new dictionary
Of post covid communication

One other thing – if I need some "same old same old"
I know I still have a phone book and an iphone
I can call old friends and buddies
And find a once pure, true, reclaimable
Form of social elation

Get Me Out of Here

What to wear
How to do my hair
Shall I wear makeup
When folks can only see a hint of me
Not a full view
Nothing but a squint of me

I wear a mask outside
And want to sidle up to folks and say
"This is a stickup"

At home – who sees me but two dogs and my best friend
Even my family is seven months quarantined from me
We resort to that squint
for a hint of what everyone used to be

But –
Zoom –
The dressing room

At least in part
Coifing from the shoulders up
Is a new form of art

Actually –
When I style myself for a zoom call
I fantasize that I am getting ready
For a dance hall

Like Studio 54
A religious service that used to sometimes be a bore
Except for perusing what everyone wore
Or who everyone was with
Or who everyone was checking out
I cry, I laugh I pout
And cannot wait until I can go back OUT

Park and Bark

So my bicoastal life suddenly became LA specific
I got diagnosed in LA
And that is where I have had to stay
Who wants to get on a plane anyway
So what do I do with myself today
I cannot stroll up Broadway
To my local merchants
Walk by and genuflect toward
Teachers College on 116th Street
Where I learned so much
About human behavior, health and wellness, mindfulness and right living
That place was so giving
Nothing like my New York walk exists in Los Angeles
Wait – what?
Yes I do have a dog
An emotional support dog
My parents died back to back not that long ago
That doggie saved my life
And he has the same coloring as my dog hating mother
She would like her grandson that she never knew
I know he's only a shih tzu
16 pounds before I give him a haircut
But he can run with shepherds and mastiffs
100 pound doggies with jaws of destruction
He can steal a rubber ball from the best of them
I think he was a soccer player in his former life
He has those powerful haunches and he is fast
All I have to do is call Lyft
Get off at old Malibu Road where I see Nanette's car parked
She's my doggie docent
My Malibu Mama
We just park and bark
And boy, there is nothing more liberating than
Running with canines
Except maybe just plain barking

A cry, a plea
A sound of confusion, or celebration or glee
And nobody comes near me
When I bark spontaneously
Anywhere
I think the neighbors think I have turrets
When all I really have is the privilege of running with pets.

I'll Cry If I Want To

Mom – welcome home from New York
Did you like the casserole I left in your fridge?
Didn't want you to have to worry about groceries
And you sometimes forget to eat
You are too skinny
Yikes now I sound like GG
Your beautiful Mom always worried about your compact figure
Maybe she wanted you to be a big girl like she was
Oh well –
What?
You found it bland?
That casserole was full of ground jalapenos
And God knows what else
I know you pride yourself on having an asbestos tongue
Wait – my husband the good Jewish doctor says that we have this new virus
    floating around
They've been talking about it on the news
Fever, nausea, debilitation, body pain, inability to breathe
Those are the symptoms
And they are about to release a warning that
Loss of taste and smell could mean that
You have it
See if you have it
Go to UCLA and get a test
I can set it up for you.

Honey – I do have it
But a mild case
I cannot see you guys
For weeks
I need to stay locked in my house
Lucky that I am right across the street
Maybe we can wave through windows
Exchange signs of love if not breath
Gosh – I'm miffed that I didn't get to see you when I came home
I need to hug you
And I've been told that hugging might be off the menu for now
For how long? Could be infinite
Wow – the inability to hug my only family
Takes me right back to the last big tragedy of my era
9/11
Remember when the New York Times featured a front page article
Condoning and even encouraging public crying?
I'm ambulatory
And I promise to stay away – from everyone –
But I think I'm going to the corner of Barrington and National
My own four corners
Starbucks, Whole Foods, Chase Bank and my hair salon
I'm going to stand in the middle of the street
I'm going to cry my eyes out
Maybe my tears will wash away illness
Baptize me for what has got to be a better future.

JENIFER WINTERS O'NEILL

*"ShiftPoetry has awakened the writer in me in a simple
and therapeutic way. My favorite part of the experience is
listening to others read their prompted poems.
I am moved every time.
Thank you Barbara and Howard."*

Jenifer is a woman who has worked extensively in media. Over the past ten plus years, she has focused her energy on her family and her community. She is very active in her sons' schools and has been a focal point for other parents in her community that have been dealing with the fallout from this pandemic. In the past six months, she has dealt with the deaths of young people by suicide as well as by a drunk driver, cancer, and illness related to COVID-19. ShiftPoetry has been a reminder to Jenifer during these trying times that she is powerful and does not have to give in to the forces of darkness.

I Have a Dream: Of Cleaning My Attic

Silly it might sound
For such a dream to abound

But I must say
It is true
I want to rid my life
Of stuff
No longer new

I think that clutter has
Clouded my mind
And I want it again
To be sublime

I really do want
To lighten the load
Not fear tossing things
From my abode

Alas I now not only have
Junk of my own
But from Mom
Stepdad and Dad

Some I'll keep
Some I'll toss
I know it may feel
Like a loss

But clear my brain
Will hopefully be
When the attic floor
Once again I shall see

Time Is Not on My Side

Time, Time, Time
Isn't on my side

Yes I spend less time
With others in groups
So I should have more time
To myself
But this isn't the case

With a school age child
Virtual learning every other week
My moments alone are limited to
The very few hours
That he is in school
And everyone else is at work

So when I do
Get an hour or two
What do I do?
I like to call my friends
And family
As I can enjoy a few minutes
Of privacy to speak at will
Without the fear
That someone will overhear
This is a rarity
And one that I hold dear

What else do I do with
A moment or two
When I don't have to worry
About what I need to do?

I play Words with Friends
That's what I do.
It keeps my mind active
And challenged and sharp
Sometimes I have eight games
Going at once

Often I will just
Enjoy my quiet house
Sit on the porch
Hug my dog
Watch the Rachel Maddow I recorded from the night before
Fast forwarding through the commercials
Or read Heather Cox Richardson's latest post
With the round-up of the previous days
Outrageous happenings in our history

Time alone is still a luxury for me
It isn't on my side right now
I know one day it will be
For now I think I'll take these few precious moments
that I've chose to write this poem
finish it
and take a nap.

The Embrace is The Place

The place I miss the most
Is in the arms of another

Besides my immediate family
I miss being
In the arms of dear friends
And loved ones

It pains me
To greet a friend
Especially one who is grieving
Or in pain
And not be able to give a hug

Even to greet a friend
With sheer joy
To be in their presence
And no hug
That's the place I miss the most

We do virtual hugs
And fist bumps
Wave or blow kisses
It's just not the same

For with an embrace often comes
Words whispered in an ear
Comforting words
A special moment of human connection
That cannot be replaced

This is the place
I miss the most

The embrace is the place
I miss the most

JESSE PUDLES

"ShiftPoetry is important to me because it has taught me to believe in the power of my own words. As an actor I have spent the 20 plus years of my life telling other people stories. While that is something I am very passionate about, ShiftPoetry has given me the opportunity to tell my own stories in my own words. Also, the fact that it is all done in the span of a two hour class means that I have no ability to overthink or over edit. ShiftPoetry reminds me that the process of creativity can be more about creating and less about making something perfect. And when we truly release into our own creative spirit, what we create can be even greater than the product we initially envisioned. ShiftPoetry has helped me to develop confidence and venture outside of my comfort zone. My evolution was made possible through my experiences with ShiftPoetry."

Jesse is one of the early, and one of the younger, participants in ShiftPoetry. He has committed his life to helping others enjoy "adult play." Jesse is in the process of launching "Spotlight Therapy," a performance workshop based around creating spontaneous egoless performance, to reintroduce the joy and healing power of performance back into people's lives. His honesty and truthfulness is a breath of fresh air at a time when others are building walls. Jesse is a leader in ShiftPoetry's LGBTQ initiative.

Rejection

Damn you, it's so obvious, rejection. I went out on a date and I got rejected, again. I've been designing my perfect man in my head, what he looks like, how he talks, his vibe. So, one night I matched with this guy on an app, met up with him and guess what . . . he wasn't the guy, not by a long shot.

He was more nervous than I expected. He was balding. He had these goofy glasses. I thought cool, the pressure is off, not my type. Then as we walked, I noticed his muscles rippling under his shirt. I talked and he listened. I opened up and shared stories. He turned out to be a great listener. He asked questions. He continued to inquire deeper into my stories, always wanting to know more. He shared stories from his old life. Deep personal stories. I began to listen and find him endearing.

As we continued to share information, I learned that we had diametrically opposed views of the world. I trust the universe and believe in the law of attraction. He has no faith in a higher power and puts his faith instead in logic and reason and people. Happily, he was never argumentative or combative.

As we approached his car, I thought we were surely headed for a good night kiss. Nothing more, just a signifier that he, at the end of the day, chose me, physically and emotionally, at least just for a moment. I definitely didn't think he was my forever guy, or even boyfriend material, but he could've been my kissing confidant. If nothing more. It's just confirmation that even though you don't feel like something is going to build, you feel enough interest to break the seal and complete the evening with a kiss. Just a kiss, is that so much to ask? I continued to ask myself that question as I watched his car drive away.

Places

Not a place, places. I miss Broadway and going to the theater. I miss rock gyms, pools, giant mansion parties, clubs and bars.

I miss the adventure of life. Of getting out of a Comedy show at 1 AM and your friend says, "let's go to an After Hours." You get there and it is completely different than you expected. Live freestyle rappers rap over a crazy beat of drum and bass. You see a cute boy in tie-dye and decide to go for it; you end up spending the whole next day with him.

It's the leap from place to place. Not knowing where you will end up next. And other places yet to be explored. Before COVID, I was planning a trip to Brazil. Before COVID, I was planning on going to an open gym at a gymnastics gym. I was going to get back on the giant trampolines and do the backflip and the twists. Before COVID, I could see musicals live and in person, marvel as the stage moves around the performers while they sing or cry or laugh. That all was BC, "Before COVID."

But for now, I'll just have to wait, and visit those places in my head.

Mantra

Ooh, where to start. Thinking, thinking, thinking. Aha, I know where to start. I am going to share my mantra. *I am the creator of my own joy.* So how did I come up with this realization?

Well, I am in a leadership program with some friends. One of the classes was on "trust." A bunch of us from the class decided to go on a camping trip. On the trip, one of my friends asked me what was coming up for me in the class.

I apprehensively stated, "Well I don't trust any of you and now I just told you." My head went into a wild tailspin; my friends are going to leave me; I'm no good. I wondered why I didn't keep my mouth shut. The negative thoughts kept on coming, blah blah blah blah.

Later that day, a different friend helped me realize why I didn't trust my friends. She helped me see that it was because I didn't trust myself. She asked me what was I afraid of happening? I said, "Saying the wrong thing." She asked, "Who decides if you say the wrong thing." I told her, "I do." She then asked, "So what are you really scared of?" I said, "No one paying attention to me."

She continues "OK, so who would you be if you didn't need attention?" I shut down. I had never thought about that as an option. She would not let me off that easy. She said "I want you to try something today: try saying *I am the creator of my own joy.*" I did and the magic that occurred for the rest of the day from taking on that mantra was nothing short of miraculous!

I acted differently that day. When my friends asked me to go on an excursion to the waterfall near where we were staying, I chose solitude. For the first time in my life, I chose to be with myself.

I spent the first part of the day searching for comfort. I was outside and it was hot. I spent hours trying to find comfort. Whenever I was able to find relief from the heat, even for a moment, I repeated my mantra, *I am the creator of my own joy*. The mantra itself was extremely comforting.

Continuing on my hunt, I happened upon a car seat that we had removed from my friend's van. I spied the perfect spot in the shade where I could lay on it; however, the heavy car seat seemed much too heavy for me to carry over to the shade on my own. Once again, I repeated my mantra, *I am the creator of my own joy*.

Like an innate wisdom washing over me, I realized that if I lifted one side and moved it, and then the other side, I could slowly lift it across the campsite. I accomplished my goal and comfortably leisured in the shade, watching as my friends were returning from their excursion.

Laying on the seat, blissfully in comfort, I continued to repeat my mantra, *I am the creator of my own joy*. As I repeated it, one of my friends heard me, and said with a gleeful look in her eyes, "I am the creator of my own joy too, and I want you to do dishes." I saw that she did not feel guilty about choosing not to do something she did not want to do. I respected her for that, and I did the dishes.

As the evening wore on and my friends continued to return, I listened to their conversations, never relenting on my chant. Then, a moment came, a moment for me to claim my power, but I felt uncertain. True, I was the creator of my own joy within my own space, but how would my joy translate to others? As I began to take ownership of my space, I remembered certain facts surrounding this weekend. I had created all of this. It had been my idea to go on a camping trip; all of these people were there because of me. I truly was the creator of my own joy. And in that moment, my friend reminded me, we had been planning to celebrate my birthday for some months before COVID hit, and he said, "no better time than now." And right there and then at that campsite, my friends sang happy birthday to me.

So, I guess the mantra is true. *I AM THE CREATOR OF MY OWN JOY*.

Standing Up For Me

Hi Jesse, you're alone again, what's going to happen?

Are you going to sing and dance?

Or maybe you are going to find a new series or maybe brain drain by simultaneously playing a game on your phone and watching TV so your brain has no space for the dark thoughts.

The thoughts that are so dark and mean that you didn't think yourself capable of them, and guess what, they are all directed at you.

You are so mean to you it's unacceptable.

Jesse, if I were your friend, which I am, I would stand in front of you and say "stop treating my friend like that, he's not hurting you, stop being so mean, he doesn't deserve it! I don't deserve it!"

I am standing now as a declaration of self-love. In *A Star Is Born*, Lady Gaga says if you're in a room of 99 people and only one of them believes in you that is enough.

Why can't that one person who believes in you be you?

Let's take that one step further: if . . . you're in a room of 99 people and only one person believes in you and that person is not yourself, you are shit out of luck. All of the fame, adoration and success cannot keep you from the truth, you don't like you.

So I am making that declaration here and now in the presence of the 11 people on this zoom call, *I believe in me, I love me, and that's enough!*

Hello World

Hi,

My name is Jesse and I am a creative Light Worker, I am on this earth to bring peace, healing and harmony.

At this moment my main modalities for that are in reintroducing play into adulthood and performance.

I want to be more mature but I never want to grow up, that is the trick that people say you have to grow up.

Who was I when I was a child you may ask?

I was carefree, I spoke my mind, I did what I wanted to do. I played games, put on puppet shows, and made up dance routines.

Who am I today?

Same person. Now I just play in a world of higher stakes and that is where the universe comes in.

I don't want to play differently because the stakes are higher, I tell the universe what I want and then I go back to playing the game for fun, not for profit.

I let the universe worry about the details and it always provides.

I often need to just let go and then let the universe work it's magic.

By the way, who are you?

SUSAN CAMBIGUE TRACEY

"ShiftPoetry has definitely got me back into writing. I used to write poetry regularly since I was a child. When I met my husband, Paul, I gave him a book of my best poems that I had created—typed and illustrated by me. He hated every poem in the book—did not accept the gift graciously—but rather with strong feelings that all poetry should rhyme!! So—I abandoned writing poetry for around 30 years—only writing a few things secretly. That is until Howard pulled me into ShiftPoetry. Now I am writing again thanks to ShiftPoetry."

Susan is a dancer, teacher, creative artist, who has worked her entire life to bring beauty to life either through her body or through her words. During the pandemic, she has not slowed and continues to teach and to be a student of human behavior. She has been an avid supporter of ShiftPoetry.

Alone Time – Too Much?

Alone time is good for my soul.
I had a lot of alone time when I was growing up
This helped me develop interests and hobbies.
Then as a student, teacher, mother and wife,
I had almost no alone time.
I craved alone time –
to feel who I am without the energy of others
bouncing in, out and around me – at times binding me.

There was never enough
Alone Time
My time belonged to my work, to dance, my husband, children,
parents and friends.

Then . . . my work declined.
My parents died.
My husband – the father of my children – and I divorced.
A single mom – I had even less time alone.
Years passed . . .
I remarried, embracing two more children.

There was absolutely no time for myself.
Shopping, cleaning, preparing meals,
going to games and concerts, homework, family trips.
Year by year, my children grew up,
Appropriately, they left our little home,
Seeking adventures and
Starting families of their own.

I retired from one career and embraced another.
Requiring more training, more teaching, more marketing.
We became grandparents –
All of our children living long airplane rides away.

My free time became weddings, births, travel time, grandmother time,
a whirl of new activities,
concerts and school performances .

I thought I just loved being active – no down time for me –
Unless it was recovering from an injury or operation –
There were a few.

Unplanned time is a waste –
I continued to have a rigorous schedule of teaching,
Counseling, working as an arts administrator,
Designing and implementing workshops,
Yoga, Pilates, being with friends
We built a yoga studio.
I scheduled more classes.

During my marriage, my husband invited me into his garden,
Asked me to share afternoon tea,
Lured me to listen as he played his guitar and sang.
I interrupted my schedule to accept these gifts –
Even if there wasn't time.
I carved it out of my busy schedule.

THEN

Seven months ago, the COVID-19 Pandemic hit –
one week after a series of four parties
to celebrate my 80th Birthday.
My birthday season was the entire month of February!
My daughter came to visit for a week –

THEN – BOOM!

Lockdown!! Schools canceled, businesses closed.
Our world changed to
Zoom meetings and Masks!!!
We were told to stay at home –

No teaching, or taking yoga classes.
No more driving to work; we now work from home!
No need for beauty treatments.

        WE CAN ALL GET SICK! SOME MAY DIE!
                 WHAT A SHOCK!
                 WHAT A CHANGE!!

Now I have time alone.
Time to enjoy things without a schedule.
At first I tolerated it!
I felt like a racehorse at the starting gate –
full of tension ready to burst forth at the sound of a gun!
I couldn't relax into nothingness.
I kept myself mentally and physically prepared
 to spring into action.
I was wired for action –
not for stillness and quiet.
I didn't want to be alone!

                      NOW

I am learning to enjoy taking time to
Breathe more fully –
I don't mean as yoga practice
But anytime during the day.
I stop and consciously breathe.

I enjoy my husband's garden – at unscheduled times,
Sit down and slowly sip a cup of Tumeric tea.
My brain has enjoyed the break,
Allowing me to create outside a timeline.
Time has stretched out –
But feels more fleeting.
And, rather than being bored,
I have become more curious and lighthearted.
Off the grid.
Time Alone is now well spent!

An Overabundance of Time – Alone!

Seven and a half months of alone time –
More than I've had
in seven and a half years!
I feel like a hamster
Running quickly on his wheel –
Staying in the same place.

All the things on my check list
– except cleaning –
Are checked off – in red ink!

Sooooooo,
I embarked on an archaeological dig
Into my life – this life –
Which seems like a few thousand years ago –
Finding relics from my past

Time to read journals written decades ago –
The same issues over many years now.
Boxes of faded photos – some surprising –
Some familiar – some seen with new eyes.
How many photos do I need?
Want?
Feel obligated to keep?
Memories creep into my mind
I play out the melodies of my life on an emotional accordion –

Images of myself in recent,
But seemingly ancient times.
Years have passed,
Yet, people remain the same in photos.
Some who appear before me are dead.
Smiling at the camera.
They are alive in my heart.

I see my two daughters,
Only a few days old – yet four years apart.
I see each of my grandchildren –
Soon after their births.
I see myself as a baby,
In my mother's arms.
We could all be toddlers together –
Different settings – different times

Next, we are all teens –
Only our clothing and posture
betray the truth –
Different eras – different styles.

In my personal digging,
I see all of my family as young,
Dreams shining in our eyes.
All on a quest
– different adventures
Made possible – or necessary –
By different events, cultures and inventions.

Being alone for longer than I wanted has given me a gift –
Dig up and examine
The treasures and lessons of my earlier life –
Challenges given to my generation became opportunities,
Disappointments and encounters

COVID-19 is a bleep in time –
Enforced alone time
Was seen by me
As restrictive punishment –
Something to endure.

In writing this poem,
I realize extra Alone Time is a gift –
And, I am finally unwrapping it.

We are in the COVID-19 Pandemic!

This is when it counts.
This is when I am reaping the benefits of choosing a playful partner.
He actually said early on that I have made him more serious about life.
If that is true,
Then, he has made me more light-hearted.

Yes,
I still aspire to set challenging goals,
Bold and rigid deadlines.
But, I have more fun in the process!

My life partner takes my hand and leads me out to his garden –
There are miracles happening here in the dirt.

He shows me humming birds and bees,
Even a snake!
He points out the yellow butterflies flitting around the Golden Wonder tree.
He transports me into a world that he designed –
Full of beauty, wonder, change,
And a large family of lizards.

He picks bouquets of flowers
From his garden – grown from seed,
Places them in a Hint water bottle at the bottom of the staircase –
I feel special as I descend the stairs.

I enter his office, and he shows me jokes!
He takes pleasure in making me laugh.
We sit across from each other at meals
Taking turns reading "Dear Amy" letters.
We take time to hear people's problems,
Then sincerely try to think what advice we would give them.
Guiding their choices to create a happy life –
Like we have.

My husband finds humor in just about everything –
But,
Does not make fun of people or their situations.
He is like a tall Garden Gnome who shyly smiles at you,
From under his hat,
Letting you know that whatever happens,
He will do his best to support you.

He is strong of character,
But doesn't impose his will on others.
He cries when something touches his heart.
He plays games of all types to keep his mind alert.
I don't like playing games,
But I do like playing house with Paul

YES,

This is when it really counts to have a playful,
Kind and loving mate.

First Save Yourself

Can anyone save the world?
Can anyone save themselves?
Can anyone save another?
Should they?
What is a truly selfless act?
What is an act of courage?
Heros don't see themselves as courageous
They do what is required – without thinking of themselves.
Angels don't see themselves as special –
They are kind, caring and act compassionately
When they see a need, a pain, a challenge –
They give everything required
Without thought of reward or self.

What is a truly selfless act?
What is an act of courage?
Acting swiftly, without thought of consequences,
Righting a wrong in a moment in time.

When you give and deplete yourself, is this healthy?
When someone demands your fealty without question or thought,
Is this morally right?
Some people become slaves,
No matter their gender, skin color, ethnicity or age
Falling under the spell of power and might.
Some people expect others to follow them without question –
dictators, crime family dons, professors, doctors, police, some parents and spouses.

There is a difference between compassion and control.
When being controlled or controlling others,
One abdicates responsibility to stay true to their moral code.
They give their power away.
Compassion is a sympathetic awareness of others' distress
and a desire to alleviate it
Personal responsibility and good choices are empowering.

My father was a combination of control and compassion.
However,
At the end of every situation
Compassion would win out.
It was this delicate combination of domineering strength, compassion and
Unwavering belief in me to always do the right thing.

He gave me the tools to save myself
and courageously navigate my own life.
He had strength, kindness, tough love, a booming voice
And a moral compass that always pointed to True North.

RUTH WAYTZ

"Thank you for bringing ShiftPoetry into existence! Pre-COVID, we did this together, eight or 10 of us to a room. I was always amazed by the courage and honesty from those trusting strangers. I was also impressed by how beneficial these sessions were to all participants. I'm a professional writer, but ShiftPoetry makes writing accessible and truly groundbreaking for everyone. People who arrived saying, "I'm not a writer" left with new confidence about their ability to use words to identify and work through some pretty deep issues. It's not professional therapy, but unlike therapy, this is available anytime and anywhere."

Ruth has degrees in English and Advertising and has earned a living through writing and editing. She won an Emmy for her work on Jeopardy!, has a broad range of clients, and her expertise crosses many fields. She comments that editing is "what you meant to say, not what you said." Ruth was one of the first to join the ShiftPoetry community. Her honesty and ability to access her feelings add to the safe environment that people experience during our workshops. Her experience as a writer enables her to articulate feelings that are not always freely accessible. We are honored to have Ruth as one of our growing ShiftPoetry family.

Giggles

I've been known to get the giggles –

Oh sure
There's regular laughing,
But this is different –

This is getting stuffed in a barrel
and heaved over Niagara Falls
or rolled down a hill at top speed
in a Persian rug.

The more you shouldn't
The more you must

Your arms and legs fly off
in all directions –
Head down
Chest heaving
Tears streaming

Yeah, you quit breathing a while back,
But it's still So Goddamn Funny!

Please Read and Agree to My Terms of Service

I recently re-watched *Mommie Dearest*,
And while I doubt anyone aspires
To emulate Joan Crawford's parenting style,
You certainly can't argue with
"DON'T FUCK WITH ME, FELLAHS!"

And guess what? Ain't my first rodeo either.

Life's. Short.

And I won't waste it on bullshit.
I'm not for everyone –
But what you see is what you get. Really.

I bring the A Game
And I expect nothing less from you.

The past is over –
Yours and mine –

Be real. Be present.
Be honest. Be kind.
Be available in joy.

Now.

Because I'm done settling.

DENNIS WEBB

"Poetry is surprising to me.
Something about meter,
and the occasional rhyme
that takes me to a sweeter place,
for which I rarely make the time.

ShiftPoetry for me is just that,
leaving the place of long drawn-out thinking
that I reside in most of the time,
and shifting to a space of intuiting instead
a story that I didn't "know"
but certainly did.

I discover myself, simply.
I bring out truth that I know, after all
one short line at a time
illuminating things large and small.

It is simple, it is profound.
It takes a form that asks for a little writing,
but enters and takes me to a place
where I visit myself, spontaneously inviting
me to be in a newly creative space.

ShiftPoetry is surprising to me."

Dennis is an engineer turned valuation expert. He is an author of books in his profession, a speaker, a leader, and a future thinker. Dennis is a visionary, an avid hiker, knowledgeable about and dedicated to fitness and health, and he's a superior tango dancer! When, during the pandemic, he broke his arm in a freak accident, which he reframed as a lesson and a message—he was thrilled that the arm was set and cast in just the right position to enhance his stand as a strong and soigne tango lead!

That Special Someone (I Hope)

Can you see me?
Can I see you?
It matters to me,
I hope to you too.

Oh, we will talk about stuff,
What occupies time,
What we do,
Hobbies and such

What we've made of life maybe
And what we expect to find next
And wax philosophically of
2020, of course

But what I really want
And I hope it's important for you too,
Is that you can see me,
and that I can see you.

The Benefits of Self-Damage

Hiking along, experiencing forest and mountains
Trail known as Beaver Brook
Whoops! Down I go. Crack!
That hurt. Fuck.

Regaining my composure almost,
Two angels appear and ask
Are you ok?
No, my left forearm is toast!

They help me make a sling
And do a quick exam,
Turns out I've lucked out,
Two ER docs, are at hand!

A bit of a healing is needed,
Surgery and all that,
A bunch-o-pain proceeded,
But humor was needed and found

I posted a pic of my arm at right angles
For a group of idled tango dancers,
And noted the fortunate position
Which I'm sure will serve me well

For the left arm remains at a right angle for dancing
And should be there and not move
The muscle memory gained
While the arm is restrained
Is the best lockdown training
I could have ever hoped for

Serious situation – anything BUT serious

It's gonna snow, it's gonna snow, it's gonna snow!
Really? Today is in 90s
Summer has been hot
Garden is cooked
Just a bit more… but Oh shit,

it's gonna snow, it's gonna snow, it's gonna snow!
Quick, cover the tomatoes,
Pot up the basil
Rosemary and fennel inside
Save the mint for Mojitos
(Priorities, people)

Welcome to Colorado!
Down into the 20s we go
Freezing what's left of the garden
Then back to summer again

No wonder all the vegetables come from California!

Happy Snappy Moments

Happy – Snappy
That was when?
Risky – Frisky
Such fun then!

Happy happens so often
Then is so easily forgotten
As I immerse in fear
And the toils of today

Was it partying in Newport?
Didn't flunk out that year, I guess.
Was it sailing to Catalina?
Nothing like the wind's caress.

Then there's Sandy Koufax's perfect game.
Just sayin'

Dancing is always good for a thrill,
Sometimes bummed, but then carried
Away for a time, immersed in love
For at least 15 minutes.

Such a long ride,
So many elations,
So many deflations,
Going for it, and getting out of it.
Rinse and repeat

How can I pick,
When the whole ride is a trip?
Grateful to be here,
No matter what comes
Thank God for my life!
And it's not close to done.

Thoughts to Ponder

There's something about forced focus,
Does a lot for self-examination
Isn't that what yogis do?

It feels like I'm being reduced
to a pure case of me
Seems I never really did know who that was,
For sure, anyway

I'm gearing up for new adventures
That have been cooking for years
They'll demand that I be
Lots more of me than I've known
At least so far

Relationships and ways of being that don't work
Had been jettisoned years ago
Who knew there was more to find?
Good Lord

Feels like I'm creating new
Maybe creating me new
But don't we do that all the time anyway?
This seems different
There's something about forced focus.

Poetry Without Pants

PART THREE:

SchtickPoetry

Satire, Spoof, and Parody

Zoom Teaching

I cannot do this,
I hate computers,
My students need to see me,
I will not use a document camera,
This is stupid,
I hate this pandemic,
Wow.
Zoom is really cool,
I can't believe it can do all this stuff,
Private rooms,
Check,
Breakout groups,
Check,
Sharing screens,
Check,
Look mom,
No hands,
I feel like a superhero,
Or at least a super geek.

© *Computer Savvy Teacher, October 2020, Who Says You Can't Teach an Old Dog New Tricks?*

How Come I Have To Wear Pants?

All I hear about is how great it is not to have to get dressed,
Everybody is on Zoom calls,
No one can see from the waist down,
No need to shave,
Who cares about what you're wearing?
Apparently my boss does,
Every workday,
The same old same old,
Nobody told me to stay home,
Why didn't I go to law school?
I guess it's cool to be an emergency worker,
I just never thought that a bagger was a first responder,
At least I don't have to worry about makeup,
Thank Fauci for masks.

© *Suzanna the Grocery Clerk, October 2020, Paper or Plastic?*

Blah Blah Blah Blah Blah

Blah blah blah blah blah,
Blah blah blah blah blah,
Blah blah blah blah blah,
Excuse me sir,
I think the passengers would be okay with you taking off your mask,
Blah blah blah blah blah,
I mean thank you.

© *Airplane Pilot, October 2020, Maybe Masks Are Safer All The Time*

Toothpaste Model

Thank you for coming,
I appreciate your commitment to my safety,
Yes,
It is patriotic and shows that you are a caring person,
I agree that more people should be so considerate,
But sometimes we have to make exceptions,
I don't think people will buy the toothpaste based on a happy face drawn on a mask,
The teeth are very white,
I guess we will have to agree to disagree,
Next,
Please . . . .

© *Frank Colgate, October 2020, Dealing with Politically Correct Divas*

Finding Love In A Pandemic

My heart was broken,
He wanted to blame me for his indiscretions,
Maybe he was right,
When the pandemic started,
I thought that it may bring us closer together,
I suggested ping pong and chess,
I talked about trips that we could take,
His heart was closed to me,
I was dying slowly,
What was the point of living with this man as he loved another?
I decided to do the unthinkable,
I would pursue romance while the world was paralyzed by COVID-19,
I went on a website,
I posted my photo and wrote about myself,
I said I was separated,

It felt good to say that out loud,
I found a man who had suffered real losses,
Two wives in less than ten years,
Like me,
He had not given up on love,
I had to convince him that I was available for anything and that I could commit to him,
My heart had been broken by my husband,
I was now intent on fixing it,
It has been a few months,
I have found love again,
I wanted only to survive this pandemic,
But I have done more than that,
I have thrived,
I no longer have to beg to be seen,
I have a man who loves me,
Who wants to be with me,
God works in mysterious ways,
I never imagined that I would be in love again,
But I am,
My husband left the marriage first,
I held on for whatever reasons,
I am glad I did so,
Had I left it earlier,
I may not have met my Don Juan,
Lightning may only strike once,
But love is always there,
You just have to open your heart,
And in 2020 during a pandemic,
You may also need to turn on your computer.

© Anonymous Snatch.com User, September 2020, Quarantine Shmarantine

Enterprising Individual

I work in the car rental business,
People weren't doing a lot of traveling during the pandemic,
Business sucked,
I watched my friends get laid off,
I wondered when my day would come,
I watched people make more money by staying home than I was making by working,
How messed up is that?
Welcome to America 2020,
I hope Putin doesn't win the election AGAIN.

© *Marvin D'Avis, October 2020, GO BLUE!*

God's Angel

I do God's work,
Many would tend to disagree,
But I am there for women when they need support,
Not direction,
The people with the Red hats are critical of what I do,
They yell out "All Lives Matter,"
But they can't even wear a mask to protect living breathing people,
I hope that if there is a God,
She is more forgiving than these White Men that use Her name like a dagger,
It breaks my heart to read about more people dying because our Federal
    Government doesn't care,
And they say I am the evil one,
I wonder what comic books they are reading.

© *Owen Meany, October 2020, Hypocrisy is alive and well and living in DC (not the comic books)*

Smash Mouth

I am a foul mouthed bully,
I enjoy making kids weep,
My shrink says that is because I hate myself,
I disagree,
I hate him,
He's a loser,
Anyone who goes for therapy is a sucker,
My mother told me that I had to change my behavior or I would never make it in this world,
She's dead and look at me,
My dad was right,
I am king,
At least that's what I tell myself every morning,
Masks are for wimps,
I'll infect whoever I want to infect,
I may be older,
But I still got it.

© *DT Rump, October 2020, Long Live The King*

Loving Routines

I never enjoyed the hustle bustle of life,
I preferred staying at home and watching TV than venturing outside,
The Pandemic started out as something I feared,
I listened to the News,
I was concerned about how my life would change,
Fortunately quarantine works for me,
Some people like drama,
I like mine served on Netflix,
It's sometimes hard being me,
But other times it's a breeze,

© *Harry H. Ermit, October 2020, Just leave the mail at the door*

Quiet Days

Before the Pandemic,
I was reinventing myself,
Trying to be the best I could be,
Not knowing exactly what that was,
Or even what it meant,
But many people were supportive,
Saying that I was so brave to be on this journey,
Some people loathed my freedom,
Wishing for better days,
Then the Pandemic and Quarantine,
I had all the time to figure myself out,
Still no answers,
But I appreciate the time to think,
I only wish that I could have had this time without watching so many people die,
Life is too short to worry,
Live,
Love,
Laugh,
Or at least smile.

© *Moses, October 2020, Finding My Way Out Of The Desert*

A Little Knowledge

I am a doctor,
A psychiatrist to be exact,
I know a lot of stuff,
I hear about other peoples' problems and prescribe drugs to ease their anxieties,
It's easy,
But I was not ready for COVID-19,
There are no pills to prescribe,
The virus is ahead of science and it scares the shit out of me,
I want to protect my family,
I don't care what Dr. Fauci or any of the "experts" say,
Isolation trumps masks any day,

I know what I know,
But it's what I don't know keeps me up at night,
People may think I'm crazy,
But when this Pandemic is over,
I know where I'll be,
Safe and sound at home with my family,
No virus is going to enter my space,
A little knowledge may be dangerous,
But COVID-19 is deadly.

© *Syd Freud, October 2020, They called me crazy*

Letting Go

I've had my issues with my mom,
She's not getting any younger,
And I'm closing the gap pretty quickly,
I have so much anger toward her,
This pandemic has reminded me that life is short,
Every day I wake thinking that today will be the day that I let go of my anger,
But I go to sleep still angry,
Telling myself that tomorrow will be different,
But it's not,
Am I insane?
Einstein may say so,
I prefer strong-willed,
Does that make me an Ass?
Probably,
I'll have to sleep on that one,
I hope that I find my heart while my mom and I both have beating ones.

© *Joan Crawford, October 2020, Mother of the Year*

Dream Killer

I am a documentarian,
No,
That doesn't mean I'm 80,
That's an octogenarian,
I produce movies about politicians that hold themselves out as something more than what they are,
I try to knock them down,
So far,
I have not had much success,
Some may even say that I have helped their political careers,
Perhaps I am the Norman Lear of documentaries,
What I see as evil is what others see as admirable,
I hope not,
But this pandemic is different,
I see a White House that doesn't care,
It even promotes unsafe behavior,
I just want to produce the ultimate exposé,
But I stay quiet,
I don't want to assume that other people feel the way I do,
I am doing the opposite of what I normally would do,
And the polling numbers indicate that it is working,
I will be quiet and pray,
Hopefully at least Someone is still paying attention.

© *M M Oore, October 2020, Less is More*

Madness I Say

I know too much,
I have a staff that reads through thousands of pages in local newspapers,
Just to find the article that nobody else has found,
I get totally weirded out by what I learn,
It drives me meshuggah,
How did this country fall so low?
I say all the right things,
Always being polite,
Like the First Lady said,
"When they go low, we go high,"
She was able to do it,
I don't understand how,
But it worked for her,
I'm trying,
But it ain't always easy,
I keep a pillow by my desk,
No,
Not for sleeping,
But for yelling into when this insanity is too much,
I wish I was sleeping,
Because maybe I would wake up to a better picture,
No such luck,
Excuse me while I scream.

© *R M Dow, October 2020, Where is Barry When We Need Him?*

My Private Eden

I used to live in civilization,
But I moved before all this craziness began,
Now I live far away from the insanity,
I have my own private bomb shelter,
No masks required because it's only me,
I hate the pandemic and all this loss of life,
But I am so thankful that I am not living it,
I just have to watch it on TV,
Secure in my voluntary isolation.

© *Eve Adams, October 2020, Politically Correct Survivalist*

The Loneliest Man In America

I used to read the ratings every week,
Opening weekend dollars,
Box office numbers,
Blockbuster movies,
Now nothing,
Nada,
Zilch,
Empty theatres,
No new movies,
AMC is replaced by Netflix and Hulu,
Loews has hit a new low,
The phone doesn't ring,
We got over all kinds of stuff in the past,
But we never had to deal with a Pandemic,
The Neilson Ratings don't matter now,
All people seem to care about is the COVID tracker,
Popcorn anyone?

© *MG Mayer, October 2020, Theatres for Rent, Cheap*

Flying First Class During a Pandemic

No long lines,
Parking's a breeze,
Free upgrades,
So what,
Everyone's wearing masks,
No food service,
No new movies,
Lots of space,
And more time to remember it's still the Pandemic.

© R. Brazen, October 2020, Fly Me To The Moon, Lots of Seats Still Available

Outer Space is Looking Good

The main issue with space settlements was that we would suffocate,
No air,
That was not a problem on Earth until 2020,
We have lots of air,
That seems to propel COVID-19,
So now we wear masks and have to stand away from everyone,
Perhaps space travel isn't so bad.

© J Pesos, October 2020, New Frontiersman

The World is Getting Smaller

I am twelve years old,
About to leave my tweens for my teens,
I am supposed to be hanging out with my friends at the mall,
Gawking at boys,
Instead I am locked up in my house,
For my own safety,
The computer is my only connection with the outside world,
Real people have been replaced by computer avatars,
The screen is my playground,
I went from cute to lethal gamer in the course of this Pandemic,
I never want to be locked up again,
I want to binge on my friends and not Netflix,
I want to meet strangers,
Not shun them,
I want to stop being afraid,
I want to read about stars and not about death,
I just want to be a girl again.

© *Gen Zer, October 2020, Ready to Reclaim my Childhood*

Learning to Say NO

I work for the most powerful man in the world,
I represent the law,
Others carry guns and badges,
I carry all the weight,
I am a spin master,
A fixer,
I am the Democrats worst nightmare,
I believed that I would take a bullet for my King,

The all powerful wizard,
Then COVID-19 hit,
And I watched hundreds of thousands die,
Shakespeare was right,
I guess lawyers do have a heart,
But my King didn't care at all,
Business as usual,
At least that's what he said,
I learned a word that I had not spoken since a Democrat was in office,
"No,"
"No,"
"No,"
It felt good to say no,
Especially as I sat in quarantine not knowing whether the virus caught up to me,
I was wrong,
People's lives do matter,
Maybe even Black Lives Matter,
I can't believe I said that,
Who knows?
Maybe I should update my resume,
Let's see,
"Sycophant looking for new butts to kiss,
"Open to new experiences,
"Has experience with elephants,
"Very good at kissing asses,"
That's a good start,
Maybe Joe will give me a shot,
I hope so,
I don't look very good in stripes.

© W B Arr, October 2020, *Justice for My Friends*

The Puppet Master

I am the controller,
I have the strings,
He thinks he's in control,
I just pull a string and he dances like a Russian bear,
Another string,
He can't pick up a cup,
How about a shuffle step,
The All Powerful doesn't look so powerful now,
Perhaps I'll cut my losses and watch him self-destruct,
He needs me,
Not a lot of gumption left in those legs,
He's too stupid to see who's running the show,
Sometimes I just feel like going back home,
Sitting on the porch,
And drinking some good old-fashioned moonshine,
But then I think about my secret accounts in China,
My hidden assets,
Nope,
There's still money for the grabbing,
I once was a good ole boy from Kentucky,
Now I'm just old and live in DC,
Maybe I should call Joe to see what we can work out for the future,
This puppet show is getting old.

© Moscow McC, October 2020, Compromise is for the faint of heart

Men Are Too Easy

I've been playing this game for a long time,
My daddy taught me,
Politics was darker back then,
Lots of deals behind closed doors,
Money talked,
People accepted the money thinking that they were doing good,
They were,
But they also were getting rich,
Now the doors are wide open,
Politicians aren't doing good,
But they're still getting rich,
I don't need money any more,
I climbed the ladder and am nearer to the top than any female ever was,
Maybe that'll change soon,
But I did it first,
Men talked down to me,
They pointed their fingers at me,
They asked me to get them coffee,
I didn't budge,
I'm nobody's girl,
I'm my own woman,
It hasn't always been easy but I never gave up,
Every man is a little boy looking for mommy's appreciation,
And every woman can use that to her advantage,
Even the current occupant of 1600 Pennsylvania is looking for his momma,
He calls me "crazy" and "nervous,"
I am neither,
I am the most powerful woman in the country,
And other women will follow me,
Some will do it better,
But I did it first.

© *Anonymous Female Politician, October 2020, I pray for you*

Crazy Like A Fox

I used to be America's Mayor,
Lot of good that got me,
I could not get elected to the Senate,
I played by the rules and watched other people become rich,
Not anymore,
I'm going to be the best friend to the most powerful man in America,
And I'm going to make sure that he stays atop the mountain,
If he falls,
Which he won't,
I'll be there to catch him,
No more rules,
No more Mr. Nice Guy,
If you think I was crazy before,
Watch out,
I'm just plain nuts,
Yep,
Maybe I'm crazy,
Crazy like a fox,
Don't matter to me what you think,
My best friend is the most powerful man in the free world,
And you can't hurt me,
But I can hurt you,
Truth is relative,
Watch your back,
Or better yet,
Don't,
Truth is for suckers and losers,
I'm neither,
Hopefully you can't say the same,
By the way,
My craziness is none of your business,

© *Former Mayor of Large City, October 2020, It takes a tragedy to lift great men from the ashes*

Alt Right Realities

Democrats in battleground states receive threatening emails to vote for
    Trump or else,
I am the Director of National Intelligence,
How do I spin this so that it helps my boss?
Worse yet,
My boss' boss is implicated in the intelligence,
He's not going to be happy,
Even worse,
His nemesis is speaking,
I know he's going be angry,
He's probably going to be throwing stuff,
I really like my job,
What am I supposed to do?
I got it,
I call a news conference when his nemesis is speaking,
That'll take the attention off the nemesis and allow us to direct the narrative,
I won't disclose that the emails were pro my boss,
And I won't point any fingers at Russia,
I'll say they were all from Iran,
And aimed to attack the Big Guy,
That too should make my boss happy,
I'm feeling better now,
I love my country,
But friendship trumps country any day,
Just breathe.

© *A Friend of DJT, October 2020, Friendship First*

I Got It

Every day,
I look at the scale,
I hate the number,
What am I supposed to do?
I look good in my clothing,
I know,
I bought a new wardrobe because my old stuff shrunk,
I don't know what's going on,
When I look in the mirror,
I still see the same person,
Maybe I'm a little heavier,
But that's normal,
I'm middle-aged,
And so what if the inches are adding up,
Again,
I'm not 20 years old any more,
I look good,
I can't help it that my clothes keep on shrinking,
I'm fortunate that I can buy new clothes,
And what's this BMI BS?
The doctor tells me that I'm obese,
What's that about?
BMI is just a number that is based on the average person,
Who wants to be average?
I can't take all this negativity,
I got it,
I'm going to find a new doctor,
And that scale has got to go.

© *Looking Good at 50, October 2020, What's in a number?*

Saving Princess

We are too attached to things,
Who cares about sheets?
Holes add character,
I know you liked that bra,
But she obviously liked it also,
She's young,
It's just a stage,
I can always buy you new stuff,
How would you like it if your family wanted to get rid of you?
What kind of ultimatum is that?
How can you even ask me to choose?
You really want me to make a choice,
I don't think this is right,
But the choice is easy,
Just send me your new address.

© *Crazy Dog Person, October 2020, Looking for Partner, Nudists Preferred*

Selective Hearing

Excuse me ma'am,
I believe your child is climbing on that table,
Oh,
He's very active,
I don't like to stifle his energy,
Ma'am,
Your child just ate that man's dessert,
He is so impatient,
He always wants the treats before dinner,
Ma'am,
Your son's screaming is bothering the other patrons,
He has such a beautiful voice,
Or so I'm told,
With these Airbuds,
I just can't seem to hear anything,
Ma'am,
Your table is ready,
Please follow me?
No thanks,
The park was closed,
And I just needed Timmy to blow off some steam,
Toodles.

© *Carol Brady, October 2020, Motherhood is Bliss*

Red is My Color

I love red,
Always have,
Probably always will,
When I was younger and trying to figure out politics,
I saw red everywhere,
Red hats,
Red states,
My favorite football team was the Redskins,
I turn red just about the color,
So I had no choice,
Blue just makes me sad,
I live in the corn belt,
So we don't have a lot of ocean,
Nope,
Blue was not my thing,
So I became a proud card-carrying Republican,
And I just love the hats,
Did I happen to mention?
Red is my favorite color,
I don't get what those Democrats have against China,
That President Zhe gets it,
So does my main man Donnie,
A man of the people for the people that count,
God Bless Mr. President.

© *A Very Average Republican, October 2020, You got me at Red*

There's More to Life than Money

I grew up kind of privileged,
I got great grades in school,
I had music and dance lessons,
Whatever I wanted,
I got,
Then I went to college and met people that were not as lucky,
It wasn't because they were dumb or came from bad families,
They just weren't white,
I realized that this country was far from great,
And for a lot of my friends,
It wasn't even good,
I am a proud woman,
The only party that seemed to fit for me was the Democratic party,
Go AOC,
Bernie was right,
Things aren't perfect,
And change doesn't happen quickly enough for me,
But at least one party sees that "greatness" is ahead of us,
And not in the rearview mirror.

© *A Woman Who Cares, October 2020, AOC in 2032!*

Apples and Apples

I don't understand how people can be so certain of things,
I look at a menu and my mind swims,
Chicken or fish?
Maybe tonight I feel like red meat,
I think that's why I became a vegetarian,
Politics is just as confusing,
I hear them speak and I don't see any difference,
I like something about each of the candidates,
Maybe I'm just too nice,
I don't understand why people are getting so upset.

It's not like anything ever really changes,
All Presidents are the same,
Sex scandals,
Check,
White,
Mostly check,
Male,
Check,
They are not like me,
Perhaps if a pansexual Eurasian American Gender Fluid individual ran,
I could get psyched,
Until then,
Menu please.

By A Person Who Does Not Like Boxes, October 2020, Tonight I'm Definitely Feeling Tofu

What It's Like to be a Person of Color in 2020

I walk through the streets,
I cross when I see a person coming toward me without a mask on,
It is frightening,
This disease that seems to feed off people like me,
People of color,
It doesn't matter,
Rich or poor,
We have a higher risk of dying,
So I cross the street and hold my breath,
Hopeful that I will not become a statistic,
I live in a white neighborhood,
I arrived,
But now I wish I was back in the old neighborhood,
Safe from danger,
Surrounded by people that cared enough about me to wear a mask,
People who really understand danger,

In the hood,
It was gangs and poverty,
Now it's rich white folks who think it's not their problem,
Wrong,
If we're all gone,
Who's going to be left to serve the Master?

© *A Person Who Wants a Better America, October 2020, Black Lives Matter*

Civility Presidential Style 2020

MODERATOR:
Today we are hosting our last and final debate,
The candidates have been informed of the rules,
My first question is to Mr. President,
What are you going to do about the Pandemic?

PRESIDENT:
Fake news,
There is no pandemic,
Everyone is out to get me,
This "flu" is overstated,
The real problem is his son,
Do you know that his son is an alcoholic?
Now that is horrible,

MODERATOR:
Thank you Mr. President,
Mr. Vice President,
If elected,
What will you do about the Pandemic?

VICE PRESIDENT:
Thank . . . .

PRESIDENT:
You see,
He can't even answer the question,
He couldn't even raise his children,
How can we expect him to manage this nation?

VICE PRESIDENT:
As I was about to . . . .

PRESIDENT:
Does a cat got your tongue?
You make me sick,
You and your cohort are responsible for everything bad in this country!!!

MODERATOR:
Mr. President,
Please let the Vice President answer the questions.

PRESIDENT:
Former Vice President,
Did I mention that his son worked for a corrupt firm in the Ukraine?
All while the "Vice President" was looking the other way . . . .

MODERATOR:
If you continue,
I will have no choice but to mute you . . . .

PRESIDENT:
Fake news,
Quiet the people,
Good folks walk into the Michigan Capital Building legally carrying weapons,
And the news goes crazy,
Where is the news when crazy people run wild in DC?

MODERATOR:
The people ran in DC because the attorney general ordered the marshalls to fire tear gas on them so that you could have your photo op . . . .

PRESIDENT:
Are we back to that story again?
What about the emails?
The missing 33,000 . . . .

VICE PRESIDENT:
Mr. President,
That was in 2016 when you were running against Secretary Clinton,
It's 2020 and your issue is with my son . . . .

PRESIDENT:
So you acknowledge there is an issue,
Aha,
Debate over,
I win,
Nananana,
I win,
You lose,
Nananana . . . .

MODERATOR:
Mr. President,
I apologize,
But I am going to mute you now . . . .

VICE PRESIDENT:
Madam Moderator,
He just took off his pants and he is mooning me . . . .

MODERATOR:
I'm sorry Mr. Vice President,
But we cannot turn off the video,
That is not part of the agreed upon rules.
Moving forward,
What do you plan to do about Russian Interference in the elections?

VICE PRESIDENT:
Madam Moderator,
He is now going full Monty on me . . . ..

MODERATOR:
Thank you Mr. Vice President,
Your time is up,
There you have it folks,
Neither candidate seems to be interested in answering the questions,
We will be back after this brief commercial interruption from our sponsors AARP, which says that just because you're old and maybe a little demented, there's no reason why you can't be President of the United States.

© *Russian Debate Transcriber, October 2020, God Bless America*

The Presidential Election – A Dog's Eye View

I sit as the humans watch the TV,
Amazed at what I see,
Too old men speaking in tongue,
I don't know how all this begun,
One is old and grey I see,
The other orange like a Bee,
I growl loudly at the ogre,
His whiny voice turns up my fur,
The other one has kind eyes,
I wonder why the orange one sighs,
Could it be that he knows what others see?
A yellow-haired liar on TV,
But the kind one looks down at the hour,
Perhaps he would like to walk and smell a flower,
Humans I do hold dear,
But I am glad I have no fear,
Climate change I do abhor,
I love my walks to the store,
But when hurricanes arrive,
We dodge the leash and instead do drive,
So if you ask me who I choose,
I will tell you after I snooze.
Bow wow,
Arf arf,
And all all that jazz,
Dog Lovers Rule.

© An Independent Thinking Dog, October 2020, Don't You Take Out That Dog Whistle

INDEX

Abunassar, Nicole 20
Altshuler, Jeffrey 4, 48
Braxton, Dorian 19
Cobbett, Jo 11
Diftler, Phoebe 37, 54
Durkin, Patrick 39
Fletcher, Stefanie 6, 60
Garcia, Esmeralda 26
Georges, Kat 15
Giri, Aseem 5
Heffler, Pam 73
Hollander, Jeffrey 19, 78
Kaguri, Twesigye Jackson 82
Kern, Howard 10, 20, 26, 86
Keshner, Casey 40

Kitt, Ava 36
Kono-Wells, Grace 94
Liao, Tara 40
Ligeti, Barbara 100
O'Neill, Jenifer Winters 109
Pace, Kermit 18
Patterson, Pat 8
Pudles, Jesse 114
Sims, Emily 20
Tracey, Susan Cambigue 120
Wadler, Pam 9
Waytz, Ruth 129
Webb, Dennis 132
Weber, Alexandra 43

ACKNOWLEDGEMENTS

Special thanks to a cherished triumvirate—Jeffrey Hollander, Jeffrey Altshuler and Kat Georges, who, even without Zoom, keep us focused!

—Howard and Barbara

About ShiftPoetry™

Howard Kern is a corporate attorney. He earned his JD with High Honors from Benjamin N. Cardozo School of Law and was an editor of and published author for the Cardozo Law Review. He also has a BA in Business Administration from Rutgers College.

Howard is the author of numerous articles and short stories, including the award winning "Who's Going to Plumb the Toilet." He also is the author of a memoir, *Walking with Kerry*, about a strong friendship that began with two men walking their dogs, and concluded with Kerry's succumbing to ALS, though he remains Howard's Guardian Angel to this day. With partner Barbara Ligeti he has created ShiftPoetry™ and co-authored *ShiftPoetry in the Time of COVID-19*.

Barbara Ligeti has been a performer, spokesperson, writer/director, producer, and coach, in various media. She also is a holistic health counselor certified by the American Association of Drugless Practitioners. At Columbia University—along with her double major in psychology and theatre—she was trained at Columbia Teachers College as a corporate and private coach. She has also been trained in mindful meditation and Kundalini yoga. She has certifications in nutrition, dance therapy, and Movement for Autism, and is an acknowledged Pilates historian and master practitioner trained by Joseph Pilates' muse, Romana Kryzanowska, with whom she created educational films to preserve the original work.

Barbara is co-author with Howard Kern of two ShiftPoetry publications, and she has written content for film, television and video. See barbaraligeti.com

www.ingramcontent.com/pod-product-compliance
Lightning Source LLC
Chambersburg PA
CBHW030000110526
44587CB00011BA/917